Sex, Gender and Disabili~~ty~~
in Nepal

This book explores the sex lives of women with disabilities in Nepal, showing that many women suffer more than men despite prevailing disability policies that emphasize nondiscrimination against people with disabilities. It also argues that far from general perceptions of women as asexual, women with disabilities are capable of leading highly creative and fulfilling sexual lives.

Using critical sexual theory and postcolonial studies as critical frameworks, the book investigates the narratives of authors with disabilities, exploring policy gaps and the need for supportive gender and sexual policies through the words of those affected. In particular, the book analyzes five female Nepali authors with disabilities: Radhika Dahal, Jhamak Ghimire, Sabitri Karki, Parijaat, and Mira Sahi, demonstrating the need for supportive gender policies to address the emotional and psychological needs of women with disabilities. Overall, the book argues that disciplinary discourses in practice often consider sex or sexuality as taboo, barely recognizing women in the context of marriage and family, and therefore creating gaps between policies and marginalized narratives.

This book provides important insights into sex and disability within the context of the Global South, and as such, will be of interest not only to researchers working on Nepal but also to scholars across gender studies, disability studies, international development, and postcolonialism.

Tulasi Acharya holds a PhD in Public Administration from Florida Atlantic University, Fort Lauderdale, Florida, USA. Originally from Nepal, Acharya has a master's degree in Women's Studies and a degree in Professional Writing. His research interests are disability, policy, gender and sexuality, marginalized narratives, critical theory, and postcolonialism, including creative writing and translation.

Routledge ISS Gender, Sexuality and Development Studies

The *Routledge ISS Gender, Sexuality and Development Studies* series explores the diverse ways in which topics of gender and sexuality relate to international development, both in theory and in practice. The book series aims to publish 'classical' gender, sexuality and development themes – such as the sexual and reproductive rights policy debates on population and sustainable development, adolescence and sex education, and policy on abortion – together with cutting edge work on embodiment, queer theory and innovative strategies of resistance to hegemonic discourses of sexuality and gender. The book series will pay special attention to the role of intergenerational power relations and how they interact with different gendered understandings of sexuality at diverse stages in the life cycle.

Wendy Harcourt leads the international editorial board with her colleagues from the renowned International Institute of Social Studies of Erasmus University, The Netherlands. The Board welcomes book proposals from researchers working in all geographic areas with special interest in research undertaken from feminist grounded theory and with marginalized groups in the global South and North.

To find out more about how to submit a book proposal, please contact the Development Studies Editor, Helena Hurd (Helena.Hurd@tandf.co.uk) or Wendy Harcourt (harcourt@iss.nl).

Teenage Pregnancy and Education in the Global South
The Case of Mozambique
Francesca Salvi

Sex, Gender and Disability in Nepal
Marginalized Narratives and Policy Reform
Tulasi Acharya

For more information about this series, please visit: www.routledge.com/ Routledge-ISS-Gender-Sexuality-and-Development-Studies/book-series/ RSGD

Sex, Gender and Disability in Nepal

Marginalized Narratives and Policy Reform

Tulasi Acharya

Routledge
Taylor & Francis Group

LONDON AND NEW YORK

First published 2020
by Routledge
2 Park Square, Milton Park, Abingdon, Oxon OX14 4RN

and by Routledge
52 Vanderbilt Avenue, New York, NY 10017

Routledge is an imprint of the Taylor & Francis Group, an informa business

First issued in paperback 2021

British Library Cataloguing-in-Publication Data
A catalogue record for this book is available from the British Library

Library of Congress Cataloging-in-Publication Data
Names: Acharya, Tulasi, author.
Title: Sex, gender and disability in Nepal : marginalised narratives and
    policy reform / Tulasi Acharya.
Description: Milton Park, Abingdon, Oxon ; New York NY : Routledge, 2020. |
Series: Routledge ISS gender, sexuality and development studies | Includes
    bibliographical references and index. | Summary: "This book explores
    the sex lives of women with disabilities in Nepal, showing that many
    women suffer more than men despite prevailing disability policies that
    emphasize non-discrimination against people with disabilities. It also
    argues that far from general perceptions of women as asexual, women
    with disabilities are capable of leading highly creative and fulfilling
    sexual lives. This book provides important insights into sex and
    disability within the context of the Global South, and as such will be of
    interest not only to researchers working on Nepal, but also to scholars
    across gender studies, disability studies, international development, and
    postcolonialism"—Provided by publisher.
Identifiers: LCCN 2019022876 (print) | LCCN 2019022877 (ebook) |
    ISBN 9780367358792 (hardback) | ISBN 9780429344060 (ebook)
Subjects: LCSH: Women with disabilities—Sexual behavior—Nepal. | Women
    with disabilities—Nepal—Social conditions. | Disability studies—Nepal.
Classification: LCC HQ30.5 .A32 2020 (print) | LCC HQ30.5 (ebook) |
    DDC 305.9/08082—dc23
LC record available at https://lccn.loc.gov/2019022876
LC ebook record available at https://lccn.loc.gov/2019022877

ISBN: 978-0-367-35879-2 (hbk)
ISBN: 978-1-03-209021-4 (pbk)
ISBN: 978-0-429-34406-0 (ebk)

Typeset in Times New Roman
by Apex CoVantage, LLC

Contents

Preface

In 2015, I was employed as a residential manager for an organization Independent Services Network (ISN) for people with disabilities in the United States. This position gave me many opportunities to interact with people with disabilities and to learn to better understand them. While working, I began to suspect some loopholes, even within the organization that worked for people with disabilities, in the way direct support professionals were involved in the lives of people with disabilities and/or in the way these professionals were trained. My job was to make home visits to individuals with disabilities, observe the condition of the homes in which they lived, and communicate with the individuals regarding their level of comfort in the home and their relationship with the home providers. I then reported on or discussed the situation in biweekly meetings at the office. One of the most unaddressed aspects of the individuals' quality of life was their desire for sex. The organization ignored or tried to avoid the issue by using labels such as "appropriate" or "inappropriate." Neither direct support professionals nor home providers were trained or encouraged to be knowledgeable of how to deal with individuals regarding their desire for sex or how to discuss sex with them. From my perspective, the topic of sex seemed to be taboo, when it came to the lives of people with disabilities who appeared to be wrongly deemed "asexual."

One of the statements I heard from one of the individuals who I supported one day when the staff called out was "inappropriate." She said, "I want to marry and wanna have sex." I did not know how to respond to her statement. The organization did not have any policies concerning sex nor was the topic discussed in the organization's meetings. I began to wonder about the condition of women with disabilities in a patriarchal society in which sex is considered extremely taboo. Originally from Nepal, I decided to research the condition of women with disabilities in the South Asian context, especially in Nepal, as well as how policies address these conditions and vice versa.

Agencies and policies to support people with disabilities, especially women with disabilities, do exist. However, whether these agencies and policies interfere with basic human needs, hampering the ability of these individuals to engage in marital and other relationships, is unknown. In this book, disability policies and the narratives of disabled women in the context of the Global South, especially in Nepal, are analyzed to understand the policy needs of women with disabilities and assess whether changes in administration and policies can better serve them by empowering them and enhancing their quality of life. This book relies on textual narratives, meaning already published writing by Nepali disabled women, government documents, and existing disability policies to inform the analysis of Nepali disability policies and of the Convention on the Rights of Persons with Disabilities (CRPD), which has been ratified by more than 160 countries.

Narratives are a vital source of useful information for qualitative analysis. By considering them, gaps among perception and reality can be investigated – meaning, differences between how disability policies view and address people with disabilities and how people, especially women with disabilities, view themselves (Feldman, Sköldberg, Brown, & Horner, 2004; Griffiths & Macleod, 2008). There are relatively few published resources that address narratives of the disabled in the Global South, and those that exist only marginally reflect on the conditions of their lives and related policy issues (Dhungana, 2006; Malhotra & Rowe, 2013). Thus, this book helps develop an understanding of how such narratives inform existing disability policies in the Global South, in general, and in Nepal, in particular, and how policies inform the condition of the disabled. Thus, this book, directly or indirectly, also includes policy questions relevant to policy makers, managers, and staff within organizations working with disabled individuals who are concerned about their rights and needs. This book also aims at reaching out to academicians, researchers, and students who are interested in gender and disability, sex and disability, disability and policy, and critical theory and postcolonialism.

Acknowledgments

I could not imagine completing this book without the unflagging support and constant motivation of Dr. Arthur Sementelli. He energized and encouraged me to write, rewrite, and revise until my writing became clear. He not only inspired me but also motivated me to focus on what I needed to do. To be honest, without Dr. Sementelli, my study of public administration theories and concepts would be a far cry from reality. Most important, I learned about critical theories, one of the foundations of my book. He made me pause where I stumbled to contemplate the problems of writing and organizing research in the course of exploring knowledge. His insightful comments, creative and critical ideas, well-thought-out reviews, professional experience, and ceaseless backing and interventions strengthened my writing. From his down-to-earth examples, I was always able to add to my knowledge.

Similarly, I deeply appreciate Dr. Fred Fejes and Dr. Mary Cameron, who remained very insightful throughout the writing of this book. Their critical feedback helped me immensely improve the quality and rigor of this study. Dr. Fejes provided me with clear direction and encouraged me to focus rather than just work hard. As a specialist on the condition of women and the marginalized of Nepal and Nepali culture, Dr. Cameron was extremely helpful in suggesting where I could gather information and made useful comments.

I am very thankful to my parents, who worked hard and showered me with love. My wife, Kripa, remained encouraging, motivational, and supportive; without her, I would not be where I am today. My two sisters, Tara and Binita, always motivated me to continue my research.

The support I received from my friends, especially Kumar, is much appreciated. Dr. Kay Traille's steadfast support and academic assistance throughout my higher education career was filled with love, respect, and encouragement. Her guardianship played an instrumental role in my dream coming true. It would be unfair if I did not also mention Dr. Rivka Felsher, who helped make this draft readable, clear, and cogent. Her kind, encouraging, and supportive work helped me achieve my academic voice in this book.

Again, I am extremely indebted to my Routledge editor, reviewers, editorial boards, and all those with whom I worked for this book to come out. I am very thankful to women authors that I have cited in this book as they gave me their permission to use their writing for research and publication. I am at a loss for words to express my gratitude, admiration, and respect for everyone who helped me with this book. I also appreciate all my professors who directly or indirectly helped me arrive at this stage of my life. In their honor, I promise to continue moving forward while keeping their advice and support in mind throughout my life.

1 Introduction

In this book, I have chosen to study the literary works of five individuals in the South Asian country of Nepal in the context of the Global South. I believed Nepal, representing the Global South, is an interesting case for inquiry into policies for disabled women for several reasons. First, the country has a multiethnic and caste-based patriarchal culture. Second, the 2015 earthquake in Nepal left many people disabled. Third, there was a substantial disabled population in Nepal prior to the earthquake. Many of the women with disabilities. Disability intersects with gender, culture, ethnicity, and sexist social attitudes in Nepal. The culture of sexism in Nepal (Acharya, 2005; Dhungana, 2006) begins with disparaging women as inferior and minimizing their lives. Sexism is even more pronounced in relation to disabled women. The plight of disabled women is framed by the sociocultural and sexist attitudes that restrict many women in South Asian countries, such as India, Nepal, and Bangladesh, from exercising their individual freedoms, such as making independent decisions and engaging in work beyond domestic tasks (Acharya, 1987; Sharma, 2007).

In developing countries, the lives of disabled women are hampered by gender issues and other social structural problems, such as the denial of land rights to women when compared to men, the neglect of women's contribution to family, and the social attitudes of preferring a son to a daughter (Forum of Women and Law Development, 2006).

In the context of India, Groce (1997) asserted that disabled women's lives "are often even more severely curtailed in much of the developing world, where poverty and traditionally negative attitudes toward women and disability are widely, although by no means universally, found" (p. 178). In a society where sons are preferred to daughters, a daughter is, so to speak, already disabled (Hans & Patri, 2003). When "the daughter is already disabled, such practices may be more pronounced, placing female children with a disabling condition at even greater risk for increased illness, multiple disabilities, or even death" (Groce, 1997, p. 180).

This problem exists even in the Western context. Disability programs in the United States affect women and men with disabilities differently (Schriner, Barnartt, & Altman, 1997). As disability intersects with gender, women with disabilities may suffer more than men with regards to the benefits they receive (Ingram, Schneider, & deLeon, 2007). In such situations, "without more insights in those complex relationships, it would be difficult to address problems of disabled women in any nation" (Schriner et al., 1997, p. 2). Thus, it is important to explore the sexed or gendered lives of women with disabilities in relation to their government.

Research has shown that women with disabilities lack political and social power in comparison to men with disabilities in the Global South (Acharya, 1987; Dhungana, 2006). Women are inherently viewed as different from men due to negative social and Hindu religious beliefs (Acharya, 1994a, 1994b, 1994c; Acharya, 2005). When women are disabled, they are seen to lack the qualities of motherhood, which is an important empowering role in the context of the Global South and especially in Nepali society. A woman who has given birth to a son and who can perform household and, often, farming chores is perceived to live a more meaningful life than women in general in Nepali society. A meaningful existence for women is defined in terms of motherhood and their capacity to have children and care for family. This is particularly the case for women from high-caste families and lineages whose remunerated labor outside the home may be viewed less favorably than that of lower-caste and ethnic women (Cameron, 1998). The social value ascribed to women who are wives and mothers influences people's attitudes toward them and can further marginalize women with disabilities who experience barriers to marriage and motherhood. This dynamic reflects how disability intersects with gender and reinforces the need to discuss gender and sex in the context of the Global South, especially in Nepali governance, to better understand the policies and practices affecting the lives of women with disabilities.

Women with disabilities in the Global South experience high rates of poverty, negative stereotypes, and gender discrimination that exacerbate their physical disabilities, thus restricting them even further (Dhungana, 2006; Lamichhane, 2014; Sharma, 2007). Such social barriers for women with disabilities are costly to the women themselves, their families, and the greater society because these barriers limit disabled women's free access to development of their capacity.

The Constitution of Nepal (2015) and Nepal's disability governmental policies guarantee freedom from discrimination based on gender as well as discrimination based on disabilities. Nepal is also a signatory of the UN Convention on the Rights of Persons with Disabilities (CRPD), which addresses the sexual and marital rights of the disabled, along with other rights (United Nations, 2006) (see Appendix A). However, the New Era for National Planning Commission (2001) showed that there are few effective strategies to implement disability policies in Nepal and in other South Asian countries.

Nepal: a case study

The Constitution of Nepal (2015) covers fundamental rights. Part 3, Article 18, discusses the right to equality. This section declares that there should be no discrimination against people based on physical condition, language, marital status, race, color, personal opinions, and disability. Article 39, Clause 9, provides state protection and facilities for people with disabilities. Article 42, Clause 3, emphasizes the rights of the disabled to live a life of self-respect and guarantees equal access to public facilities. The Disabled Protection and Welfare Regulation (1996) and Protection and Welfare of the Disabled Persons Act (1982) include provisions for different services and facilities for persons with disabilities, such as educational rights, health facilities, employment opportunities, self-employment facilities, tax exemption facilities, travelling facilities, and free legal aid services. Dhungana (2006) and the New Era for National Planning Commission (2001) highlighted physical impairments and called for improvement of disability-friendly infrastructure and employment services for people with disabilities. However, the policies barely recognize women in the context of marriage and family. Further, research has yet to focus on the personal concerns of the disabled, including the understanding of the disabled women's social lives and the need to develop policies related to gender, sex, marriage, and motherhood.

An underlying problem in developing appropriate policies is disability prejudice in Nepali society. People view disability as the result of a sin committed in a past life, that is, as destiny (Sharma, 2007). Those who entertain this attitude assume that people with disabilities are incapable of or unfit for marriage and motherhood. The takeaway from this is achieving an understanding of the social, psychological, and cultural experiences of people with disabilities, and reflecting upon these understandings in policy making could reduce the problems faced by disabled women in their daily lives (Bernert, 2011; Bernert & Ogletree, 2013).

In Nepal, different political and historical upheavals bring about changes in policies and agencies' roles in addressing the lives of women, as well as female empowerment and discrimination based on sex and gender (Acharya, 2017). However, there appears to be little progress in ameliorating the conditions of women with disabilities (Acharya, 2017). In this book, I investigate the potential mismatches between disability policies and the experiences of women with disabilities from Nepal as a case study to reflect and inform similar disability and policy situations that may exist in the Global South or around the world.

Theoretically, in this book, I have considered both critical theory and postcolonial studies as tools to assess the narratives of disabled women to determine whether policies and the agencies working for people with disabilities in Nepal are useful, consistent, and informed by, or inform, disabled Nepali women's narratives. Critical theory and postcolonial studies frame this analysis of literary works by disabled Nepali women. Foucault's (1990) views of biopower, biopolitics, and sexuality can help the reader better understand disability and gender-sexuality in the larger social, historical context of Nepal. Postcolonial studies compliment critical theory because postcolonial studies establish intellectual spaces for marginalized people to speak for themselves and balance the imbalanced "us versus them" binary power relationship between colonists and colonial subjects (Said, 1979; Spivak, 1992, 2010). In a postcolonial context, colonists are those who deem themselves able, and colonial subjects are those who are disabled. Spivak (2010) and Said (1979) discussed the roles of power and knowledge that name, define, and control subjects. These ideas also relate to Foucault's (1990) concept of biopower (defined later), and the naming, defining, and controlling of subjects. These concepts are discussed fully in Chapter 3. In this book, I also use Riessman's (2008) and Barthes' (1975) narrative methods focusing on thematic and structural analysis of the text, study symbols, and metaphors to generate meaning, for sensemaking, and to make the implicit explicit.

The purpose of the book

In this book, the focus is on understanding disability and disability policies in Nepal and on informing disability policies in the context of the Global South. It intersected the experiences of women with disabilities; sex and gender; caste, culture, and social beliefs; and how these factors impact women with disabilities and the disability policies designed for them. The purpose of the book is to:

- explore the meaning of disability and gender policy in the context of Nepal and the Global South;
- analyze current Nepali disability policies and CRPD as revealed through the literary works (narratives) of disabled women; and
- inform policies through personal narratives, specifically, literary works (Griffiths & Macleod, 2008).

Typology of narratives

In this book, literary works of disabled women are reviewed alongside disability policies. Autobiographies, biographies, and creative works by people with disabilities that inform disability policies to draw on their life stories, their life histories, and the stories of their sex lives were analyzed (Griffiths & Macleod, 2008). They were classified into four different categories to critically analyze mismatches of policies with select narratives of disabled women using the following typology (see Table 1.1). I have used Nepali disabled women's narratives and Nepali disability policies as a case study. This typology can be a good model for any researcher in any context, most possibly in the South Asian context.

Intelligible and empirical

These are the narrative texts of people with disabilities. The narratives look reasonable, measurable, logical, coherent, concrete, and objective, and they seem to make sense to policy makers. The narratives in this category are related to the physical difficulties and problems with which disabled people must cope. They appear to be clear, explicit, and deal with issues that can be addressed easily. The possible solutions relate to policies that address infrastructure such as disabled-friendly facilities and public places, as well as employment opportunities and working conditions for the disabled.

Empirical and observational

These are governmental policy texts formulated for people with disabilities. They are logically and rationally formulated with specific objectives. They are designed to offer guidelines to the public in clear language. These policy narratives are largely formulated based on a "one size fits all" concept. Different governmental and nongovernmental disability organizations and institutions implement and enforce these policies. They mostly view policy as a means of empowering people with disabilities both economically and politically through education and employment. These policy narratives are guided by measurable, calculable, and scientifically objective rationales. They are directed toward tangible results such as providing services and facilities and removing physical barriers that may directly impact the lives of the disabled. The policies aim to address the concerns of the intelligible and empirical category.

Interpretive and heterogeneous

These narrative texts express the complexities inherent in the experiences of disabled individuals, revealing often hidden oppressive conditions. The narratives may provide neglected and subjective perspectives, including a range of experience unfamiliar to many readers. These experiences may exceed the general knowledge of the able-bodied and help policy makers

Table 1.1 Typology of narratives: typology testing

	Individual narrative texts of the disabled	*Policies for the disabled*
Empirical	I Intelligible: Logical, coherent, not complex Possible to understand the individual's narratives easily Example: "If I have to go to the hospitals of Nepal, they are not disability friendly" (Ghimire, 2014, p. 26).	II Observational: Policies that can be tested or observed Example: "The Act will provide different services and facilities for persons with disabilities, such as educational rights, health facilities, employment opportunities, self-employment facilities, tax exemption facilities, travelling facilities, and free legal aid services" (Disabled Protection and Welfare Regulation, 1996, p. 4).
Interpretive	III Heterogeneous: Narrative texts based on/coming from perspectives of different caste/race/culture/gender, and different contexts Complex, incoherent, difficult to understand Examples: "Actually, all humans have the matter of sex, and no one can be separated from it. It is because I also have youth and adulthood. To be without sexual feelings is to be a person without emotion" (Ghimire, 2014, p. 36). "I bloomed like pear and guava plants in full bloom, like the blossoms of rhododendrons and marigolds" (Ghimire, 2014, p. 77).	IV Reflexive: Policies that discuss or reflect on the gender or/and marital issues of people/women with disabilities A question of research?

develop more broadly responsive policies. The narratives may appear abstract, subjective, and heterogeneous. The personal narratives of people with disabilities likely intersect with caste, ethnicity, gender, and sex, and they may bring different subjective perspectives to the attention of policy makers. These are examples of personal narratives evoking the lived experiences of disabled people, which often go unacknowledged by policy makers. They are mostly the thoughts and feelings of people with disabilities communicated through experiences. These narratives may be more abstract and difficult to translate into implementable policy. Individual thoughts may contest accepted norms and values of society. The significance of these narratives is implicit. This may contrast with explicit narratives in the intelligible and empirical category. These personal narratives may contain many allusions, metaphors, similes, symbols, and ideographs, which are mostly found in poetic expressions that are complex in nature and may require interpretation to be addressed.

Interpretive and reflexive

These texts are policies that reflect on or discuss gender and marital issues in relation to women with disabilities. They are very significant for research to explore if disability policies address the concerns of the interpretive and heterogeneous category. The study of this category might have a significant impact on future policy texts. Here, I have analyzed and interpreted individual narratives from creative works by people with disabilities. A critical narrative analysis of the words, images, allusions, metaphors, and ideographs inform interpretations of what the writers expressed, assessing if the issues have been addressed in disability policies. If there are policies addressing the issues in the interpretive and heterogeneous category, how effective and clear are they? Or have women with disabilities defied the existing disability policies? If so, how and why? It is here that hegemonic power may come into play at the intersection of gender, caste, and culture.

Significance of the book and its contribution

The book contributes to both critical theory and postcolonial studies in the context of disability and gender policy studies by assessing the narratives of people with disabilities within the context of disability policies in Nepal and in the Global South. This book may justify the use of critical theory to explore gender and disability by policy makers, as well as reveal the importance of narrative analysis as a method to analyze the lives of the disabled. The findings of this book could be used to discuss and generate clearer, more sensible policies to address the lives of the disabled. Most significantly, the book underscores the importance of gender policies in the lives of people with disabilities.

Quality of life is possible by establishing good governance and serving people through the execution of policy (Wilson, 1887). Policies that affect the welfare of marginalized people in society and could help identify particular policy problems with the hope that, by recognizing those problems, the government can efficiently and successfully remedy these policies.

Good policies intend to achieve the betterment of society and people and to use its "energy toward performing for the people being served" (Ashworth, 2001; McSwain, 2002, p. 8). Good policies serve the marginalized segments of society, such as women and the poor (Denhardt, 1999). They address marginalized communities and citizens who are deprived of government services, and the necessity to serve them (Hood, 1989; Wettenhall, 2003).

If a state fails to serve its people through public institutions, it cannot improve the quality of people's lives. By bringing disability policies and disabled women's narratives into discussion, this book can contribute to future administrative practices, including formulating or implementing targeted disability policies on behalf of disabled women in Nepal, in particular, and in the Global South, in general. As suggested by Wilson (1887), improving the condition of people, specifically women with disabilities in this context, via better policy formulation and implementation is part of the mission of public administration, a "systematic execution of public law" (p. 212). To address the condition of women with disabilities through policy making and its proper implementation, public policies can play a role in the betterment of conditions for marginalized people. This book answers the following questions:

- are there clear policies that address the sexual/gender/marital lives of people with disabilities, particularly women?;
- what are the life stories of people, especially women with disabilities, and the stories of their sex lives?; and
- how do disability policies reflect on the narrative texts of women with disabilities and their sex and gender and sexual orientations?

Organization of the book

This book is organized into eight chapters. Chapter 1 discusses the background, context, and significance of this study, and introduces the questions the book answers. This chapter also provides why the author was interested in the study of sex and disability and in writing this book. This chapter helps the reader understand why the study was important and identifies the possible takeaways.

Chapter 2 provides an overview of disability, gender, and social construction theories. It also surveys research on gender, disability, and policies, including issues, agendas, and problems that are similar and different in both developed (i.e., the United States) and developing countries (i.e., the Global South, especially Nepal). This chapter provides a brief overview of disability conditions in different contexts, disability models, and people's attitudes toward people with disabilities. This helps one understand the ongoing problems faced by disabled people, how gender intersects with disability around the world, and the need for research to explore such issues and address them.

Chapter 3 elaborates on critical sexual theory and postcolonialism addressing disability and gender and sex. This chapter provides an overview of critical theory and postcolonialism and describes how these theories are important frameworks for analyzing the life stories of individuals. In this chapter, there are detailed discussions of Foucault's biopower so as to better understand the lives of people with disabilities and of Spivak's concept of subaltern and Said's colonialism to help better understand the lives of people with disabilities. This chapter helps explore human freedoms that are linked to people's quality of life.

Chapter 4 explains the qualitative narrative research method employed in this study. This chapter highlights the structural analysis methods of Riessman (2008) and Barthes (1975) and their use in the analysis of the narratives of disabled women. This chapter defines the narrative method and explains its significance in understanding the lives of women with disabilities. The chapter shows how the data were collected and how they were interpreted. It discusses four types of narrative analysis and how these stories help us gain a better understanding of human lives.

Chapter 5 discusses the narrative texts of disabled women through the lens of critical and postcolonial theory. This chapter shows how women with disabilities in Nepal are able to deconstruct the idea that disabled people are deemed asexual. It also presents various stories and autobiographical works written by women with disabilities that show their ability to reflect on the significance of desire. The chapter additionally study's focus on how society views disabled women differently in a culture that is sexist and patriarchal.

Chapter 6 provides the textual analysis of disabled women's narratives in relation to disability policies. The chapter compares two different narratives – the disability policy narratives and the narratives of women with disabilities. The chapter shows how disability policies address women with disabilities and how the narratives of women with disabilities inform policies. It also discusses the Convention on Rights of Persons with Disabilities (CRPD) and how the treaty is insufficient to address the sex lives of women with disabilities.

Chapter 7 tests the typology of narratives and discusses the findings. The findings show how disability policies and the narratives of women with disabilities mismatch. Chapter 8 presents the conclusions of this study. This chapter mainly reviews the whole discussion in the book, providing a concise summary, useful information for future researchers in the field, and takeaways.

2 Disability and policy problems, gender, and social construction

The term *disability* garners negative cultural and social associations such as ugly, old, aberrant, deformed, derailed, debilitated, or feebleminded. Each of these associations devalues the human body (Garland-Thomson, 1997). Garland-Thomson (1997) explained that: "Culturally generated and perpetuated standards such as beauty, independence, fitness, competence, and normalcy exclude and disable many human bodies while validating and affirming others" (p. 7). Garland-Thomson (1997) elucidated that the disabled fall under the category of "aberrant human beings" (p. 7) who fail to conform to the cultural standards of a normal body. Roest and Braidotti (2012) defined disability against the norms of socially constructed bodies, which view disability as "loss," "lack," "deficit," "tragedy," "melancholy," and "anomalous" (pp. 165–166). Hiranandani (2005) argued that disability must be understood as a construct related to prevailing economic organizations, institutions, bureaucratic structures, and political contexts in a particular historical period.

Disability and policy problems

Problems with disability policies may be prevalent around the world, but the research on this topic remains limited. A plethora of disability literature, mostly in the West, has discussed the existing laws and identified elements that make a nation's disability policy viable (DeJong & Lifchez, 1983; Ingstad, 1999; Ingstad & Reynolds-Whyte, 2007; Oliver, 1986, 1996; Percy, 1993). Western literature focuses on the architectural barriers to the progress and well-being of people with disabilities. DeJong and Lifchez (1983) stated that: "Although the rights were discussed in the law, the architectural barrier limited opportunity, promoted discrimination, prevented integration, restricted choice, and frustrated self-help" (p. 26). In the context of the United States, DeJong and Lifchez (1983) urged that policy makers need to be aware of the complexity of the population of the disabled for whom environmental accommodations are required, and policy makers should understand that disabled people are "a complex collection of individuals with diverse functional limitations" (p. 33).

The main challenge for policy makers is to understand how disabled people view themselves (Doe, 1997; Shuttleworth, 2007; Stevens, 2008). More effective policies can be developed by encouraging self-help initiatives to remove barriers and encourage disabled individuals to participate in society (DeJong & Lifchez, 1983). Traustadottir and Harris (1997) emphasized the complex issue of reproductive rights and argued for the importance of addressing structural inequality in policies. Similarly, Schriner, Barnartt, and Altman (1997) noted that policies about women's sexuality and reproductive issues should include those issues for women with disabilities. Although legislation and policy cannot address all of the problems experienced by women with disabilities, Schriner et al. (1997) recommended addressing gender issues and power relationships socially. Samowitz (2010) opposed the repressive arbitrary attitudes and policies that control and deny the basic human rights of people with disabilities. These prescriptions might be viable in the context of Nepal.

Political organization, ideology, and culture shape knowledge that translates into policy design. Ingstad and Reynolds-Whyte (2007) found that the development of rehabilitation and intervention programs by the state has been accompanied by legislation, administrative procedures, welfare institutions, medical diagnoses, professional specializations, and business interests. These legislative and administrative procedures might not take the rights of people with disabilities into account, or those rights might have been lost in bureaucratic practices (Lipsky, 2010).

In Nepal, disability policy is based on a medical model of disability emphasizing treatment and rehabilitation (Thapaliya, 2016). The provisions of services for disabled people are also discriminatory in that these provisions are not gender friendly or are ineffectively applied, and the rights of disabled women are thus violated (Acharya, 1994b; Bhandari, 2013). Nepali law, for example, allows a husband to marry another wife if his current wife is insane or mentally disabled, but the law does not address what a wife may do if the husband is mentally impaired (Acharya, 1994b, 1994c; National Code of Law, 2016). The use of words such as *crippled*, *feeble*, and *helpless* in the law is also discriminatory.

In Western contexts, disability policies emphasize equity and efficiency goals, meaning that they prioritize the optimal allocation and equal distribution of resources throughout society (Burkhauser & Daly, 2002). Burkhauser and Daly (2002) argued that policy makers should be able to balance equity and efficiency goals. The authors also asserted that disability is "a dynamic process rather than a static classification" (p. 219), meaning disability can change in breadth and severity across the life. Many factors shape disability and disability programs, includingeconomic conditions and people's perceptions and attitudes toward the disabled. Burkhauser and Daly suggested that policy makers should acknowledge disability as a dynamic process.

In the general context of defining disability and policy implication, Hahn (1985) asserted that an understanding of disability policy issues is very important. Hahn argued that the concept of disability in policy does not "seek to specify whether the problem is in the individual or in the environment" (p. 294). The policy rarely identifies the rationale for measures that are taken in reaction to the perceived advantage. Such policies also represent "an official belief that a disability constitutes disadvantageous circumstances that oblige a public or private agency to offer some type of response" (Hahn, 1985, p. 294). Despite perceived responsibility, government policy makers have "failed to exercise that obligation in a logical or consistent manner" (Hahn, 1985, p. 295). Hahn (1985) also asserted that:

> The bureaucratic drive toward parsimony, let alone the desire for effectiveness, is likely to produce an effort to reduce or eliminate the contradictions and inconsistencies within present disability policy; and decision makers are apt to expect assistance from policy analysts in this task.
>
> (p. 295)

Both the social structure and built environment are fundamentally shaped by public policy, laws, and regulation (Hahn, 1985). In addition, Hahn proposed, "The recognition that disability is a product of the interaction between individual and environment characteristics is not only an important contribution of investigators of disability policy but also a significant theoretical foundation for future research" (p. 296).

In Nepal, people with disabilities are denied many forms of expression that are essential for all citizens to participate fully in Nepali society (Bhandari, 2013; Dhungana, 2006). Bhandari (2013) and Dhungana (2006) explained that these include rights to exercise biological and emotional needs. In Nepal, so-called able-bodied people rarely recognize the disabled as capable people with both biological and emotional needs who can perform normative societal tasks (Bhandari, 2013; Dhungana, 2006). These attitudes create doubts about disabled people's capacity for, and the appropriateness of, sex and marriage in their lives, which in turn blocks their access to civil rights, disability policies, and government services.

In the context of the United States, Haveman, Halberstadt, and Burkhauser (1984) categorized programs for the disabled into two types: ameliorative and corrective. Ameliorative programs are primarily cash transfer programs, while corrective programs include vocational rehabilitation, sheltered employment, and other employment strategies, and quotas. Haveman et al. (1984) discussed what influences the design of disability policy. Those unfamiliar with disability policies are unable to see the growing challenges the world would face in structuring an efficient and equitable policy toward disabled workers (Berkowitz, 1979; Berkowitz, Johnson, & Murphy, 1976; Haveman et al., 1984).

In addition, there is a lack of effective vocational opportunities for women with disabilities. Groce (1997) argued that low-paying vocational opportunities are not effective. Aside from a few vocational opportunities and other programs for women with disabilities, no sufficient records are kept on disabilities in the Global South, and there are no strong laws that protect disabled women (Dhungana, 2006; Ghai, 2002, 2003; Wehbi & Lakkis, 2010). Berkowitz et al. (1976) and Boylan (1991) also discussed disability policy problems and suggested different social, cultural, and political models of disability. In the context of Nepal, to investigate disability policy problems, an understanding of gender issues in Nepali society is crucial.

Disability and gender

Since disability intersects with gender, it is important to know what gender is and how it is different from sex. Gender is social, and sex is biological. Although the meanings of the terms *gender* and *sex* are contested (Cranny-Francis, Waring, Stavropoulos, & Kirkby, 2003; Jackson, 1998; Ross, 1994), they tend to overlap (Beasley, 2005). Beasley (2005) explained:

> Gender typically refers to the social process of dividing up people and social practices along the lines of sexed identities. The gendering process frequently involves creative hierarchies between the division it enacts. . . . The gendering of social practices may be found . . . in a strong association between men and public life and between women and domestic life, even though men and women occupy both spaces.
>
> (p. 11)

Some have defined gender as being commonly linked to the social interpretation of reproductive biological distinction, while others have viewed and analyzed it differently (Beasley, 2005). The terms *gender* and *sex* are widely discussed across the subfields of feminist, sexuality, and masculinity studies that aim to study biological and social division, biological sex difference, sexuality, sexed identities and practices, and gender arrangements. Beasley (2005) further explained that:

Feminist and Masculinity studies tend to line up together and focus on the significance of gender (sexed identities), while Sexuality studies focus upon the organization of desire (not on having or engaging in sex per se, but upon sexualities) and are increasingly somewhat antagonistic to gender approaches.

(p. 15)

A general social understanding of gender is that gender refers to men and women and sex refers to male and female. These two different concepts, gender and sex, create categories. Gender is an outcome of sexed identities, and gender concepts are socially constructed, meaning after a boy is born, he starts being socialized with daily chores that belong to a man, and likewise for a girl. Sex is considered to be biological/natural (i.e., male and female). However, it also creates a category of male and female excluding other sexual identities and sexual orientations. According to Butler (2006), gender is rephrased to the socially constructed characteristics of masculinity and femininity that reinforce a heterosexual normative. Both gender and sex need to be discussed in a way that addresses all humans from different ethnic, social, and cultural backgrounds with different sexes and sexual orientations. In this section, the focus is on how women in general seem to be gendered.

Within the context of Nepal, the country learned about gender equality from different political changes such as the People's War, also called the Maoist Movement (1996–2006), that addressed poor women, or *dalits*, and the untouchables who live miserable lives. The movement dismantled the oppressive structure of the society that never allowed women to seek equal rights and greater autonomy (Jarmul, 2006; Nelson & Chowdhury, 1994; Yami, 2010b). One of the significant changes the Maoist insurgency brought to the lives of women is transforming what Collins (1998) called "unjust social institutions" (p. 273). These institutions include state policy, the policy of labor markets, schools, industries, banks, insurance companies, and the news media, where women were always excluded. All of those unjust social institutions were threatened by the entry of women into Maoists' militarism (Yami, 2010a). However, there still exists gender discrimination in Nepali society, showing that the country needs to do a lot of work to confront social perceptions of gender.

Gender theorist Stivers (1993, 2002) differentiated public from domestic gender to show how women have been excluded from the public realm and to call attention to their unrecognized contributions in that realm. Stivers (1993) observed that: "Both pervasively in theory and persistently in practice, the household has been viewed as the realm of women; and women's concerns, when they evolve around their domestic responsibilities, have been seen as private – not political – by definition" (p. 5). Stivers also suggested that social roles have been gender-typed. Stivers' idea of a "cult of true womanhood" (p. 111) emphasizes women's womanhood being associated with her ability to bear a child, be sexually active, work in the kitchen, and look after children. If a woman fails to perform those activities, she loses her womanhood. Stivers showed how gender roles are reflected in different institutions, relegating women to subordinate positions and preventing women with disabilities from exercising their rights.

Stivers (1993) discussed gender roles as an effect of gender images that reconfirm women's role in society. Stivers (1993) asserted that:

> The images of expertise, leadership, and virtue that mark defenses of administrative power contain dilemmas of gender. It contributes to and is sustained by power relations in society at large that distribute resources on the basis of gender and affect people's life chances and their sense of themselves and their place in the world.
>
> (p. 4)

This dilemma of gender resonates in the public administration of Nepal. Research on the participation of women with disabilities in public administration in Nepal also shows gender inequality, reflecting gender images such as those of expertise, leadership, and virtue associated with men. T. Acharya (2017) wrote that although civil service law encourages women's participation in government by providing a quota of 45% women, their participation remains minimal. The Election to the Members of the Constituent Assembly Act (2007) requires that political parties contain at least 50% female candidates, and other percentages are prescribed for additional categories such as the *dalit, adivasi, janajati*, and others. For a brief note, in the context of Nepal, gender issues are even more complicated in the sense that Nepali women continue to be seen through the eyes of high-caste Hindu women and some Newar women, and this homogenized projection of Nepali women ignores the demands from marginalized groups of women such as *adivasi* (indigenous) and *janajati* (outside of Hindu caste) (Tamang, 2009).

Stivers' (1993) concept of how gender plays a role in society, specifically in bureaucratic institutions, speaks on behalf of women in Nepal. In Nepal, gender plays a vital role in shaping the perceptions of both men and women. Their roles are defined for them and taken for granted (Acharya, 2005). If a woman has a disability, she is deemed unable to meet gender expectations. If she is disabled and of a lower caste, or *adivasi* or *janajati*, and also of a different sexual orientation, this deeply affects her participation in public society. This reinforces Stivers' concept of how women are gendered and excluded from the public realm. It also shows how public and private spheres are associated with gender in different institutions and practices, reflecting on the exclusion of women from public roles and power that further associates women with the private sphere and domesticity in which women are restricted from public spaces that are deemed to be men's domain.

Subedi (1997) wrote that the growth and development of both male and female children are shaped by social values and informed by patriarchal traditions. Nepalese society strongly prefers sons to daughters because sons are considered protectors and providers for their families (Acharya, 1994c; Cameron, 1998; Dhungana, 2006). From the moment of a girl's birth, her economic value is restricted. She is considered an unwanted addition to the family to be later married off. Since these patriarchal norms and values are center to Nepali society, there is a high incidence of gender discrimination. In this cultural context, the lives of women with disabilities are problematic (Dhungana, 2006) and tend to be tied with what Stivers (2002) called "private spaces," (p. 4) which infers the duties of housework and child-minding.

In the context of the United States, Emmett and Alant (2006) identified an "interface between disability and gender" (p. 446). Emmett and Alant asserted that scholars studying gender issues have neglected women with disabilities. Exploring the relationship between the disability and gender, Emmett and Alant (2006) observed that female disability is often associated with poverty, race, and ethnicity except that "conditions in the developing countries are likely to be worse and considerably more prejudicial to people with disabilities and especially to women with disabilities" (p. 454). Emmett and Alant noted that women with disabilities face other environmental and social disadvantages. That is, they do not have as equal access to social participation in decision making, reproductive health services, and others, due to social stigma and stereotypes.

Gerschick (2000) argued that disability intersects with gender and gender with other "social characteristics including sexual orientations, race, and ethnicity to shape the perceptions, experiences, and life chance of men and women" (p. 1263). People with disabilities seem to be treated as asexual or genderless humans. When a person with a disability is a woman, she has a different life experience due to different social and cultural attributes associated with being female.

Groce (1997) stated that poverty and negative attitudes toward women have made being a woman with disabilities more painful than being a woman without disabilities. This shows how gender intersects with other social characteristics (Gerschick, 2000). In the context of developing countries, more specifically, India and Nepal, Groce (1997) explained that: "A woman's social and economic class, her marital status, her family's social networks, her level of education, and her specific types of disability will make a dramatic difference in her quality of life and her ability to make choices" (p. 179). Groce further explained that:

> Those women who are born with a disability or acquire a disability early in life are often segregated from broader society from early childhood on, routinely confined within their homes or institutionalized against their will by families who fear public disgrace or physical or psychological harm to their daughter, should their disability status become known.
>
> (p. 180)

This plight is usually overlooked, both by groups that advocate for women's rights and those that defend disability rights (Groce, 1997). Over the years, many disability advocacy groups and rehabilitation initiatives have tended to concentrate on and be run by men (Groce, 1997). Programs that advocate for women's educational, economic, and social equality pay little or no attention to the needs of women with disabilities (Bhambani, 2003; Groce, 1997).

Dhungana (2006) and Sharma (2007) differentiated between people with disabilities in general and women with disabilities in relation to their social status in Nepal. The authors observed that women with disabilities are one of the most marginalized groups among the disabled and exist at the lowest status level. For example, they each found that women with disabilities are excluded from community and family activities, prevented from accessing entitlements available to men, and deprived of other property rights. As a result, women with disabilities are doubly marginalized both as women and as women with disabilities. Furthermore, they are over-represented among people living in absolute poverty (Sharma, 2007). They are mostly cast down, stigmatized, rejected, and excluded from family, community, and government authority (Dhungana, 2006). Dhungana (2006) argued that if a woman becomes disabled, a man can marry another wife without divorce. "Disability does not stop a man [from] doing anything unless his physical and mental disability is severe. But the situation is just the opposite for disabled women" (Dhungana, 2006, p. 23). This reflects gender bias and the urgency of further research into gender, disability, and policy making in Nepal.

The situations of many disabled women in the Global South tend to be exacerbated by traditional gender roles guided by religious principles and values. The majority of men and women seem to accept traditional gender roles in the Global South as strengths of their culture (Acharya & Bennett, 1979; Watkins, 1996). Cameron (1998) observed that:

The daughter's birth is marked by sadness and fear – sadness that a son was not born and that the life of the daughter will be difficult, and fear because she is a potential threat to the honor of her father's patriline.

(p. 297)

M. Acharya (1987), T. Acharya (2017), and Greene (2015) suggested that the deeply rooted patriarchy in Nepali society controls many areas of women's lives, obliging societal anticipations of marriage, prescribing social roles for them, and indoctrinating them in social value systems. Ghai (2002) argued that in "poor families with hand to mouth existence, the birth of a disabled child or the onset of a significant impairment in childhood is a fate worse than death" (p. 51). In a study of women with disabilities in Bangladesh, Rahman (1993) indicated that:

In a country where it can be a curse to be born a woman, the problems of a woman with a disability are fourfold: she is a woman; she has a disability; she lives in poverty; she is a victim of illiteracy and superstition. The extent to which a woman with a disability is accepted is determined by the social position of her family.

(p. 40)

Among people with disabilities, the situation of women with disabilities in the Global South is different from their male counterparts. Men with disabilities have more opportunities than women with disabilities. A disabled man can marry a nondisabled woman, but the vast majority of disabled women are forced to remain unmarried, making them a burden to family members (Addlakha, 2007; Dhungana, 2006; Ghai, 2002). The exception to this is that of a rich disabled woman. If her family provides an exorbitant dowry to a groom, then it might be possible for her to marry (Addlakha, 2007; Dhungana, 2006; Ghai, 2002; Rahman, 1993; Thomas, Prakash, Hema, & Raja, 2002). For example, in Nepal, a society where marriage is the norm for women, 80% of disabled women are unmarried (Dhungana, 2006). Groce, London, and Stein (2014) indicated that this low marriage rate compounds links between poverty and disability through lack of "dowry, bridewealth, or right to inherit property or resources generated jointly over the course of the relationship" (p. 1560). Women face double discrimination because of their disability and their gender when it comes to marriage. In this context, Ghai (2002) imparted that:

Within the Indian cultural context, disability implies a "lack" or "flaw" leading to a significantly diminished capability; images of the disabled are associated with deceit, mischief, and devilry. Disabled people are sometimes depicted as suffering the wrath of God and being punished for misdeeds. Yet another strand of this cultural construction conceives of disability as eternal childhood, where survival is contingent upon constant care and protection.

(p. 51)

Regarding structural and physical barriers in Nepal, women are likely to be more impacted by disability than men (Dhungana, 2006). Acharya (1987) and Dhungana (2006) explained that patriarchal society limits women's freedom and practices. In addition, women with low income and of a lower caste are further marginalized. The socioeconomic status of women with disabilities is low, and they lack education and employment compared to their male counterparts (Lamichhane, 2012b, 2014; Lamichhane, Paudel, & Kartika, 2014). Lamichhane (2012b) indicated that the employment situation is different for disabled women than for disabled men. Disabled women are overwhelmingly unemployed, and there is a disparity between disabled men and women in relation to job types. Liasidou (2014) observed that:

Disability needs to be understood in conjunction with issues of gender, and other sources of social disadvantage linked to race and socio-economic background, so as to advance alternative analytical lenses to challenge deficit-oriented practices and to make transparent the ways in which wider social structures and institutions create/perpetuate inequality.

(p. 159)

It is crucial to understand the importance of sex, gender, and marriage in a South Asian context, specifically the Nepali sociocultural context, to better understand the situation of Nepali women, women with disabilities, and their reflection on policies formulated to address the conditions of the disabled. Although many discussions on gender equality agree that these women deserve equal opportunity and respect irrespective of their race, ethnicity, culture, and religion (Constitution of Nepal, 2015), in a country like Nepal, there are still many religious and patriarchal challenges to equality (Acharya, 2017).

Religion, purity, and patriarchy

In the context of Nepal, the Hindu religion features a male-based hierarchy that is foundational to patriarchy (M. Acharya, 1994b; T. Acharya, 2005). The position of women in the Laws of Manu is contradictory. It says that as a girl, a woman should obey and seek protection from her father, as a young woman she should do the same from her husband, and as a widow she should obey her son, although the laws emphasize the reverence of women (Olivelle, 2005).

Gautam (2017) explained that sex and its influence on gender are consistent with the discourse of Dharma, religion "based on caste and patriarchal identity that assigned the wife the duty to offer sexual pleasure as part of her general relationship of obedient service to her husband" (p. 28). This leads to undesirable social practices such as female seclusion and Purdah, child marriages, and mob rapes of women during times of social upheaval (Acharya, 2017).

Women's honor and chastity are linked to the patriarchal ideals of safeguarding the purity of sisters, daughters, and women in general. These ideals also generate discriminatory laws (Limbu & Jha, 2018). Limbu and Jha (2018) argued that, in a patriarchal system, nationalist narratives are increasingly deployed to discourage women from exercising their rights, agency, and subjecthood as equal citizens of the state. Mostov and Ivekovic (2006) underscored that idealizing women's purity tends to leave women's bodies vulnerable. Tamang (2000) asserted that laws and policies made in Nepal reinforce the masculinized Hindu regime that created gendered citizens by naturalizing women's roles as mothers and wives. This further supports Hindu-based patriarchal narratives that reduce women to being simply daughters, sisters, or sisters-in-law who embody familial and national honor rather than identifying them as autonomous subjects and equal citizens of the state (Limbu & Jha, 2018; Tamang, 2000). These discourses of Nepali women and understanding of their bodies in terms of honor and purity tend to leave women with disabilities even more vulnerable than other women.

Cameron (1998) asserted, "The process of naturalizing caste and gender ranking in Hindu culture has far-reaching ontological and conceptual consequences" (p. 44). The caste groups categorized by the Hindu religious system, coupled with the patriarchal culture, impact women of lower castes and the *dalit*, who are often ostracized from society and bear the brunt of inequalities at home and in their daily lives.

Sex is deemed taboo in Nepali society, and women have more restrictions on them than do men. In Nepali society, marriage is deemed a gateway for sex. Sexual relationships outside marriage are viewed as sinful, unethical, and immoral (Acharya, 1987; Acharya & Bennett, 1979; Greene, 2015). Greene (2015) stated that sexual and gender minorities in particular face a deeply rooted stigma and obstacles in "virtually every arena of their lives" (p. 2), despite law that guarantees the rights of sexual and gender minorities. Different religious texts interpret what is acceptable behavior for women. At the same time, men seem to have a lot more freedom. It is not easy for a high-caste woman to remarry after a divorce due to social attitudes that she is immoral or failed to maintain family honor, whereas men are encouraged to remarry (Dhungana, 2006).

From the very origin of Hindu texts, including literature, myth, and scripture, women acting to please male figures to receive something good, useful, and generous has been encouraged, along with what women should do and should not do in society in general (Mackinnon, 2006). This is how Nepali women's motivations are created, and it has put many Nepali women in a state of psychological dependence on men (Christ, 2006). For example, the *Swasthani Brata Katha*, a Hindu mythical text, portrays the story of Goma Bramini, a 16-year-old girl, married to an 80-year-old man who is paralyzed. She spends a dozen years serving him as her husband (Birkenholtz, 2018; Nepal, 2018). In this narrative, the old man's disability is not an issue as he is a male. This demonstrates gender bias. Birkenholtz (2018) stated that although *Swasthani Brata Katha* is a piece of the women's literary tradition, it is patriarchal in ideology because it perpetuates ideals such as child marriage and strengthens the subordinate position of Hindu women.

In the end, Bramini's fidelity to her husband and tolerance is rewarded when the old man turns out to be the young Lord Siva (Nepal, 2018). This story has influenced Nepali women deeply even though the country is declared to be secular. A woman who worships Shiva or his phallus believes that her wishes, dreams, and desires to find a young and handsome husband will come true. Thus, worshipping Shiva is also a way for a woman to wish for her husband's health, energy, and longevity.

Despite stories of goddesses such as Kali and Durga, who Hindu people worship as goddesses of power or as goddesses who represent the victory of good over evil, there is not a single story that discusses a man's reverence to female figures like the ones in *Swasthani Brata Katha*. Many Hindu (both in India and Nepal) women consider their husband a reflection of the image of Shiva, and they think that worshipping their husbands is worshipping the Lord Shiva. Despite the fact that the Hindu religion has many goddesses representing goodness, power, and victory, Dalmiya (2000) argued that they have become no more than the creations of male fantasies.

There are some instances where unmarried daughters are worshipped as goddesses. For example, in the Newari religious tradition called *Kumari Pratha* or the living goddess tradition, a young prepubescent girl is worshipped as a manifestation of the divine female energy of Devi. However, she is replaced by another Kumari after she starts her period and cannot marry anyone throughout her life (Hafiz, 2017). Similarly, Bennett (1983) discussed sacred sisters and their symbolic roles, presenting two models: *patrifocal* and *filiafocal*. In the former, wives and sisters-in-law have low status, and their relationship with men is based on duty and obedience. In the latter, daughters and sisters have high status, and their relationship with men is based on affection. For Bennett, both symbolic models are empowering to women because those in the patrifocal realm will live a married life and go through motherhood while others live with their parents free and honored. However, by presenting Hindu women's perspectives, Bennett disclosed attitudes that only represent women of high caste. Bennett conformed to the idea that social structure is dominated by patriarchal ideology, which puts women in ambivalent and conflicting positions. This begs the question whether married or unmarried women are empowered. In this regard, Christ (2006) argued that:

> Religions centered on the worship of a male god create "moods" and "motivations" that keep women in a state of psychological dependence on men and male authority, while at the same time legitimating the political and social authority of fathers and sons in the institutional society.
>
> (p. 212)

Christ (2006) described a mood as "a psychological attitude, such as awe, trust, and respect, while a motivation is the social and political trajectory created by a mood that transforms mythos into ethos, symbol system into political reality" (p. 211). Religions and religious texts have "such a compelling hold on deep psyches of so many" (Christ, 2006, p. 211).

Mackinnon (2006) argued that "men have become knowers, mind; women have been to-be-known, matter, that which is to be controlled and subdued, the acted upon. Of course, this is the social matter; we live in society, not in the natural world" (p. 55). Since social norms, values, and practices are the outcomes of the superstructure of society that is represented by social, cultural, political, and religious discourses, the center of the discourse tends to be men, therefore subordinating Nepali women. Christ (2006) argued that patriarchal religion has "engendered powerful, pervasive, and long-lasting moods and motivations of devaluation of female power, denigration of the female body, distrust of female will, and denial of the women's bonds and heritage" (p. 218).

One problem with religious stories is that in patriarchal religions, gods are supposed to be all-powerful creators of the world. It has been accepted by most people in Nepal until relatively recently that the world was created by a male deity (Dalmiya, 2000). Dalmiya explained that most goddesses are portrayed as irrational, bizarre, and strange looking, although there are some goddesses such as Devi, Kali, and Saraswati that are worshipped in the Hindu tradition.

Disability and social construction

Social construction is the study of how perceptions are shaped by socio-cultural practices (Berger & Luckmann, 1966; Schutz, 1972). Regarding the social construction of reality, Berger and Luckmann (1966) stated that:

> Different objects present themselves to consciousness as constituents of different spheres of reality. I recognize the fellowmen I must deal with in the course of everyday life as pertaining to a reality quite different from the disembodied figures that appear in my dreams. The two sets of objects introduce quite different tensions into my consciousness and I am attentive to them in quite different ways. My consciousness, then, is capable of moving through different spheres of reality. Put differently, I am conscious of the world as consisting of multiple realities.
>
> (p. 33)

According to Burr (2003), social constructionism is a critical perspective of "our taken-for-granted ways of understanding the world" (p. 2). Knowledge is gained through social processes (Burr, 2003). Understanding social processes is crucial to exploring how things are taken for granted. Taking things for granted creates essentialism, and social norms are therefore seldom questioned (Ingram et al., 2007; Roest & Braidotti, 2012). Social constructionism questions the essentialism of seeing things as "having definable and discoverable nature" (Burr, 2003, p. 6). Burr (2003) explained that understandings are "not only socially constructed; they are sustained by social practices that often serve the interest of the dominant groups in society" (p. 38). Meaning is shared; categories are created within the culture, and social constructionism helps one see them clearly. The problem in the categorization of disability is that it shapes the perceptions of state support, that is, perceptions that worsen the situation of disabled women (Lamichhane, 2014). A clear understanding of these categories or biases can help one question the normative standards of society. Thus, social constructionism can be considered a challenge to oppressive and discriminatory practices in a society.

Researchers have employed the concept of social constructionism in studies to analyze the traditional social roles based on normative values in a society (Berger & Luckmann, 1966; Schutz, 1972). Socially constructed realities inform the law, and the law, at times, fails to represent the social reality of marginalized, poor, and disabled communities (Ingram et al., 2007). Regarding the view of policy makers, Ingram et al. (2007) explained that:

> The incorporation of social construction of target populations as part of policy design helps explain why public policy, which can have such a

positive effect on society, sometimes – and often deliberately – fails in its nominal purposes, fails to solve important public problems, perpetuates injustice, fails to support democratic institutions, and produces unequal citizenship.

(p. 93)

Policy makers sometimes view social constructions as natural phenomena and seldom question them (Ingram et al., 2007). People with resources have access to policy-making agendas, while the marginalized fall behind and fail to receive government services. Ingram et al. (2007) asserted that, "Widows, orphans, the mentally handicapped, families in poverty, the homeless, and many other categories of unfortunates" lack political power that "sharply curtails their receipt of benefits" (p. 103).

Ingram et al. divided the target population for public policy into four categories: advantaged, contender, dependent, and deviant. The disabled fall under the third category, dependent. However, in Nepal, people view disability not only from the dependent category but also from the deviant category, especially *dalit* or lower-caste women with disabilities, which prevents them from receiving adequate government benefits.

Roest and Braidotti (2012) theorized disability as a socially constructed phenomenon, characterizing contemporary social theory as dominated by "a socially constructivist vision of human embodiment which reduces the body part to inert matter shaped by social, cultural and symbolic codes" (p. 162). In other words, normative social standards shape one's consciousness and knowledge of the subject. Roest and Braidotti defined disability differently from socially constructed views of disability and challenged the essentialist perspective of impairment, arguing body and subjects as socially created, opening the unexplored territories of collective subjectivity, and recognizing the experiences of people with disabilities. Goodley (2013) analyzed disabling culture and its influence on "subjectivities" (p. 632). He discussed that the disabling culture shapes and influences a disabled consciousness and understanding of disability in society. The understanding differentiates the so-called able-bodied from the disabled, influencing the perceptions of the disabled themselves and people's attitudes toward them (Goodley, 2013).

These general attitudes of the disabled also shape the perceptions of policy makers. Ingram et al. (2007) reinforced that socially constructed knowledge plays a crucial role in shaping policy. It is because even in the process of defining and solving policy problems, normative societal values guide the actors (Sabatier & Weible, 2017). Coming to a solution about a policy problem requires recognizing the socially constructed, hegemonic power at play because socially constructed views among actors involved in policy design tend to ignore other dimensions or alternatives that are crucial to recognize for the betterment of the society. Ingram et al. (2007) recommended acknowledging the complexity of socially constructed views that are always inextricable, multiple, and hegemonic.

The study of women with disabilities in Nepal through their narratives may help identify and clarify socially constructed beliefs and knowledge. Regarding social construction of disability, Wendell (1996) proposed that different social factors contribute to disability:

> Culture makes major contributions to disability. These contributions include not only the omission of experiences of disability from cultural representations of life in a society, but also the cultural stereotyping of people with disabilities, the selective stigmatization of physical and mental limitations and other differences (selective because not all limitations and differences are stigmatized, and different limitations and differences are stigmatized in different societies), the numerous cultural meanings attached to various kinds of disability and illness, and the exclusion of people with disabilities from the cultural meanings of activities they cannot perform or are expected not to perform.
>
> (p. 5)

Ignoring the experiences of disabled people and taking the stereotypes of disabled women for granted may further worsen conditions experienced by disabled women. Studying the narratives of women with disabilities is important not only to explore social practices that have been taken for granted but also to question them and support efforts to free disabled women from social and cultural oppressions.

Malhotra and Rowe (2013) described disability as being socially constructed; it shapes our understanding and perception of what it means to be able-bodied. This socially constructed concept regarding ability preserves and validates what it means to be normal by limiting us to certain, so-called, normal standards (Malhotra & Rowe, 2013). Ghai (2002, 2003) identified culture as the cause of disability. Siebers (2010) introduced the "ideology of ability" (p. 7) as a way of explaining how an ideology is created in particular cultural and social contexts. Siebers (2010) asserted that if one does not fit into that category, one is considered abnormal, not fully human, different, deviant, other, and therefore disabled beings fall from the "baseline of humanness" (p. 10). The baseline of humanness has to do with the human body and the mind that "gives or denies human status to individual persons" (Siebers, 2010, p. 10). It can be generalized that the way disability is viewed is socially and culturally constructed and is reflected in policies as well (Ingram et al., 2007).

Dhungana (2006) found that stigmatization and stereotypes marginalize the disabled, particularly when people view the disabled person as having committed a sin in the past, as being bad luck, or as being diseased. Dhungana (2006) found a difference in perceptions between men and women in her study regarding the presence of disabled woman and the bad luck they bring to a community. If the disabled woman is *dalit*, they may be deemed a pariah. Ingram et al. (2007) called these stereotypes about people with disabilities myths. The mythic nature of socially constructed disability acts to marginalize disabled people. Ingram et al. (2007) stated that: "These myths become inculcated in the culture embodied in policies so that their authenticity is unquestioned, and they are accepted as fact" (p. 107).

Heyes (2015) indicated that social learning becomes cultural learning. If this is so, one also needs to question the social construction of disability. Hiranandani (2005) questioned the cultural construction of disability in general. Hiranandani pointed out the attitudinal and environmental barriers that challenge the disabled, questioned the monolithic view of disability as individual inadequacy, and challenged the traditional perspective of disability. Questioning the social construction of disability is beneficial in the context of Nepal, where women with disabilities rarely question how the general public views disability. Women with disabilities in Nepal tend to try to pass as abled or retreat from community life due to stereotypes and social stigmatization (Dhungana, 2006).

In the discussion of disability and social construction, there are many social beliefs related to disability that shape people's perceptions of viewing disability as a consequence of the law of karma, which at times remains unquestioned. The law of karma becomes the perception of disability associated with evil, witchcraft, bad omens, or infidelity (Lamichhane et al., 2014; Waldman, Perlman, & Chaudhari, 2010). Stone (2005) defined karma as a "belief that one's present life is determined by what one has done, right or wrong, in a previous existence" (p. 27). Brodd (2003) defined karma as a concept in Hinduism and Buddhism that explains causality through a system where good effects are derived from past good actions and bad effects from past bad actions. Stone (2005) asserted that: "South Asian beliefs related to disability and its causation range from those that focus on the behavior of the parents, particularly the mother, during pregnancy to sins committed by extended family members and reincarnation" (p. 27). Some people in South Asian contexts believe that disability can be caused by "supernatural agents, such as punishment from God or the curse of the devil for their sins, or those of their parents, or even their ancestors" (Stone, 2005, p. 28). Brouwers et al. (2012) emphasized the perceived stigma of disability. The law of karma can be defined as the perceived stigma of disability in this context.

In Nepali society, social stigma is deeply rooted in a religious belief in karma. From one's caste to physical features, the concept of karma interprets many dimensions of Nepali life. Belief in karma in relation to disabled women in this context is very important. The belief in Nepal and other societies in the Global South, that disability is a result of doing something wrong in the past, informs the idea that the disabled should suffer in the present. This belief makes the lives of women with disabilities even more difficult in those societies. Therefore, the law of karma in relation to religious beliefs plays a crucial role in how disabilities are understood and how lives of women with disabilities are perceived and interpreted.

Disability and sexuality

Shuttleworth, Russel, and Weerakoon (2010) stressed the significance of sexual drive as being "integral to well-being and quality of life" (p. 187). Surveys have shown that people both with and without disabilities have a general interest in sexual activity (Shuttleworth et al., 2010). Many researchers have emphasized the importance of the association of sexuality and quality of life (Giami, 1987; Nosek et al., 1994; Sandowski, 1993). McCabe, Cummins, and Deeks (2000) proposed that sexuality and quality of life are of particular importance for people with disabilities, ". . . yet the association has received almost no attention in relation to people with physical disability" (p. 115). Most able-bodied people perceive those with disabilities differently, and people who care for disabled people often "hold negative or patronizing attitudes towards sexual expressions" of the disabled as it is deemed "inappropriate" (Shuttleworth et al., 2010, p. 188).

Generally, so-called able-bodied people deem disability and sexuality to be incommensurate (McRuer & Mollow, 2012), linking disability with asexuality. Constructions of asexuality and disability have been and continue to be closely bound (Cuthbert, 2017). O'Toole and Bregante (1992) underscored the idea that able-bodied people tend to ascribe asexuality to marginalized groups, especially disabled persons. Kim (2011) emphasized the inseparable intersection of normality and sexuality. Kim (2011) proposed that disability "is an embodiment neither to be eliminated, nor to be cured, and is a way of living that may or may not change" (p. 479). This suggests that no one can change the nature of one's body, and a disability should be accepted as a different kind of ability. Rogers (2016) observed that disabled people "do not often get what they desire, for example love, marriage, and friends" (p. 619). They feel lonely and want relationships just like able-bodied people. Those who show signs of sexual needs/desires are deemed promiscuous (Rogers, 2016).

In the context of the Global North, McCabe (1999) suggested that the sexual feelings of people with disabilities have been neglected and that they are rarely granted sexual rights. McCabe's (1999) studies of sexual knowledge, experience, and feelings among people with disabilities show that the difficulty "stemmed from the negative attitudes generally held by parents and caregivers towards the expression of sexuality among people with intellectual disability" (p. 158). McCabe (1999) found that knowledge about sexuality is not provided to people with disabilities, and because "there is limited discussion about sexuality, negative feelings develop in relation to sexuality and there are low levels of expression of sexuality" (p. 168).

Stevens (2008) stated that "public policy regulating the sexual lives of people with disabilities continues to depend on the notion of disability as a deviation from normalcy" (p. 40). The author also pointed out the problems that occur when advocates for the rights of people with disabilities do not understand their sex lives. Stevens (2008) refused to see policy making as conducting "acts of benevolence" (p. 5) but rather as a manifestation of what Wilkerson (2002) called "erotophobia" (p. 40). Erotophobia is the fear of sex influences, social taboos, and social constructs that guide policies and public perception of marginalized citizens. Stevens (2008) argued that: "Marginalizing people based on their sexuality is a powerful tool of social oppression" (p. 42) that further marginalizes people (Stevens, 2008; Wilkerson, 2002). Stevens (2008) argued that negative images of disability and of the sexuality of disabled people, as well as policy codifications that define the lives of disabled people, need to be subverted and replaced with images that claim their "beauty, difference, humanity and sexuality in a way that is public and proud" (p. 46). Many researchers have suggested that the issue of sexuality is a difficult topic for policy makers (McRuer & Mollow, 2012; Shakespeare, 2000; Shakespeare, Gillespie-Sells, & Davies, 1996; Stevens, 2008). However, addressing it "provides more support for more sexuality activists and scholars to be aware of disability and other intersectional issues related to sexuality" (Stevens, 2008, p. 45) and shows how public policy might help people with disabilities to positively address their marital sex lives.

3   Critical sexual theory and postcolonial studies

Before discussing critical sexual theory, it is important to first understand critical theory. Critical theory emerged from the Marxist tradition and was developed by a group of sociologists at the University of Frankfurt in Germany, which became known as the Frankfurt School (Adorno, 1991; Habermas, 1987, 1990; Habermas & Seidman, 1989; Horkheimer, 1976). Critical theory as a tool helps study culture or literature while exploring the social, historical, and ideological forces and structures that shape or control human ideology – in other words, human consciousness. It is useful to analyze individual's life stories or narratives or any autobiographical works. The theory helps better understand society by analyzing domination and exploitation that are problems of society and exposes the power that oppresses the marginalized.

Critical theory seeks to "abolish oppression and social injustice, to promote human integrity (self-rule), individual freedom, and bridge the theory/ practice gap by reconstructing theory as lived experience" (Abel & Sementelli, 2005, p. 459). Critical theory also focuses on human values, exploring alternatives and possible solutions to problems, making it useful for public administration and public policy (Box, 2005; Forester, 1980, 1993). Forester (1993) and Kelly (2004) underscored the use of critical theory to interpret narratives in policy. Such interpretation may inform a change in the hegemonic-bureaucratic model of public administration to a more collaborative one (Kelly, 2004). Miller (2012) argued for policy inquiry as social practice by mobilizing the dynamics of democratic discourse, that is, using "historically built up social practices to enhance democratic projects" (p. 103). Critical theory highlights routes to liberty adequality, which have the potential to bring about a better life. In this regard, Abel and Sementelli (2005) asserted that "the emancipated individual pursues his or her true interests either regardless of dominant ideologies, practices, discourses, and bureaucratic institutions or in a manner highly skeptical of them" (p. 143). Critical theory aims to bring things into critical notice that are taken for granted or ignored as naturally social and cultural and that affect quality of life or marginalize one's emotional, physical, and psychological state.

Denhardt (1999) proposed that reason and freedom are achieved through the act of critique. Researchers use critical theory to recognize the tension within us, to reveal contradictions, to question false consciousness, and to find the causes of social domination in modern life (Denhardt, 1999). Critical theory provides policy makers with a methodology to allow marginalized voices – in this case, disabled women – to be heard. This chapter also discusses critical sexual theory and postcolonialism as frameworks for disability policy studies.

Critical sexual theory

Critical sexual theory is an approach that helps examine how ideas about gender and sex develop, and how and why some constructions of gender and sex become normative and oppress the sexual or marital lives of women with disabilities. Shuttleworth (2007, 2012) and Shuttleworth, Russel, and Weerakoon (2010) used critical sexual theory as a tool to investigate how gender and sex influence social perception and affect the freedoms of women with disabilities. Critical sexual theory employs critical theory to observe gendered/marital-sexual behaviors and perceptions of sexist society. Critical sexual theory, in this book, is a framework for critically examining marital-sex behaviors or gender perceptions of the disabled, especially disabled women. Defining critical sexual theory sheds light on the bases of subordination in dichotomous discourses of the sexual versus asexual categorization of disabled women.

In this study, critical sexual theory helped examine the oppression of gender, or "biopower," which is "an explosion of numerous and diverse techniques for achieving the subjugation of bodies and the control of populations" (Foucault, 1990, p. 139). The control is imposed through disciplinary institutions that are guided by certain rules and regulations and by social, cultural, and moral values practiced in society. Critical sexual theory was used to understand how biopower and other social characteristics, such as caste, culture, and gender, intersect with disability. An examination of biopower is crucial to understanding the power relationships that oppress the bodies of the marginalized, or in this study, women with disabilities.

According to Foucault (1990), discourse is not objective, neutral, or universal; rather, it is subjective, normative, and contextually specific and becomes fixed, hegemonic, and oppressive. For example, women with disabilities are stereotyped and stigmatized, which introduces the discourse that they are asexual, unfit for marriage, and feeble. This discourse oppresses them, using the power of disciplinary discourses over the body of women with disabilities (Foucault, 1990). According to the Laws of Manu, the concept of disabilities in Hindu nations compounded by the law of karma, and the duties of women, these social beliefs about gender exert power over women with disabilities and dehumanize, suppress, and oppress them (Foucault, 1990; Olivelle, 2005). These beliefs stand out as social disciplinary institutions that control, regulate, and subject the bodies of women with disabilities (Foucault, 1990). Although the Laws of Manu prescribe some obligations to honor women, it is more concerned with women's duties and obligations to men and society (Olivelle, 2005). This discourse claims the incapability of women with disabilities while exerting power over their bodies.

Foucault's (1975) "disciplinary institutions" (p. 139) can be equated to Nhanenge's (2011) "logic of domination" (p. 174), which reinforces institutional and policy practices that impinge on the freedom of individuals, causing tensions among society and individuals, and also a sense of alienation (Warren, 2000). Looking into the narratives of women with disabilities in this context, one may explore whether there are tensions between society and individuals, or between social perceptions of disability and disabled women in Hindu nations. In repressive societies, disciplinary institutions characterized by rules, regulations, rationality, and calculable results exert power upon subjects such as marginalized people, mentally ill people, women, or women with disabilities in this context. The study of the intersection of disability and gender along with other social characteristics provides opportunities to reflect on how biopower prevents women with disabilities from exercising their freedom (Foucault, 1990; Shakespeare, Gillespie-Sells, & Davies, 1996; Shuttleworth, 2012).

Foucault's (1975) disciplinary practices reveal hegemonic power that impacts marginalized people, and these practices need to be transgressed to change the socially constructed views of women with disabilities and emancipate the marginalized from the oppression of those practices. Herz and Johansson (2012) proposed that the "ambition of critical theory is to transgress and resist hegemonic practices and ideologies" (p. 528). Foucault's (1990) biopower helps examine how the government controls the marginalized by suppressing and silencing their voices. The exertion of power upon the marginalized bodies, with the help of social norms and values that define who is who, punishes those who do not fit normative standards. The lives of people with disabilities are controlled by visible and invisible forces in society. These forces include social values and attitudes, as well as preventive policies and organizations that purportedly work for people with disabilities. The rights of people with disabilities are lost as they are deemed impaired, and they are subsequently deprived of actualizing aspects of their lives, including the emotional and social. Under social domination – particularly the concept of ableism – people with disabilities have reduced freedom to be in charge of their own lives.

Foucault's (1990) discussion on sex reveals how the discourse on sex and gender is constituted in different periods of time, controlling women's bodies. Critical theory awakens us to the absences in the discourses that define, govern, discipline, or control the subject. Foucault deconstructed how the subject is shaped by biopower, making the subject a dependent entity. This relates to Adam's (2015) concept of "absent referents" (p. 50). This is the concept Adams (2015) employed to examine how animals become "absent referent" as this concept "permits us to forget about the animal as an independent entity; it also enables us to resist efforts to make animals present" (p. 50). This concept helps us explore gender segregation and discrimination due to the exertion of biopower (Foucault, 1990). Exploring biopower helps make the invisible visible, reckons discrimination against animals and, symbolically speaking, women, the poor, and other marginalized communities. To explore biopower, a further discussion of absent referents becomes imperative. Critical sexual theory plays into the absent referent of marital sex lives of the disabled. In this regard, Adams (2015) further related meat eating to women's oppression:

Eating animals acts as mirror and representation of patriarchal values. Meat eating is the re-inscription of male power at every meal. The patriarchal gaze sees not the fragmented flesh of dead animals but appetizing food. If our appetites re-inscribe patriarchy, our actions regarding eating animals will either reify or challenge this received culture. If meat is a symbol of male dominance, then the presence of meat proclaims the dis-empowering of women.

(p. 241)

One can interpret these ideas in relation to disabled women. If disabled women are deemed asexual, we ignore their body parts that take part in sexual activity, and their body parts become the absent referent that further ignores motherhood and the concept of ideal womanhood. These concepts of motherhood and ideal womanhood imply how such discourses control the subjects (Foucault, 1990).

Fraser (1985) explained that critical theory employs categories and explanatory models that reveal rather than omit relations of male dominance and female subordination. Fraser recommended critical social theory to explore gender-sensitive categories. Critical sexual theory, in this study, was employed to explore how one's marital sexual behavior or ability is the absent referent, or in other words, ignored or dominated in male-dominated or -gendered society. In such societies, women are marginalized and therefore, visibly or invisibly, controlled in the context where women are considered as, Fraser (1985) wrote:

> members of the "helping professions" utilizing mothering skills (nurses, social workers, child care workers, primary school teachers); as targets of sexual harassment; as low-wage, low-skilled, low-status workers in sex- segregated occupations; as part-time workers; as workers who work a double shift (both unpaid domestic labor and paid labor); as "working wives" and "working mothers," i.e., as primarily wives and mothers who happen, secondarily, also to "go out to work"; as "supplemental earners."
>
> (p. 113)

These ideas reiterate Foucault's (1990) discourse on discipline that discusses how disciplinary institutions control their subjects. Critical sexual theory sheds light on the debate surrounding the importance of power in the construction of sex and gender (Foucault, 1990). The categorical study of male vs. female that divides gender or sex into two categories, such as male vs. female or man vs. woman, imposes the social hegemonic power, and, therefore, constructing sex and gender in social, biological, psychological contexts. This debate can help lead to the autonomy of the marginalized (Allen, 2013; Foucault, 1990).

Allen (2013) described critical theory as a contextualized analysis of the interstices and intersections of power and autonomy through which the researcher may recognize the oppressive character of sex/gender identity. The theory can also be analyzed as an important tool through which one may find the necessity to change what we *think* about sex and gender already saturated in sex/gendered power structures that are identity constituting. For example, Agger (1993) critiqued the domination of women's reproductive activities through a male standard of value.

Narratives of disabled women reflect absent referents that expose bio-power. For example, Hindu women (mostly women from India and Nepal) are depicted in architecture and wooden sculptures in and across religious buildings as tamed and passively exploited in much the same way as are animals. Adams (2015) asserted: "The structure of the absent referent in patriarchal culture strengthens individual oppressions by always recalling other oppressed groups" (p. 69). This can be applied to all marginalized people, including the *dalit, adivasi,* and *janajati* women in the context of Nepal and India. The social structure is a disciplinary structure that tries to control and tame the marginalized subject (Foucault, 1990).

In the context of disabled women's sex lives, marital sexual aspects of women with disabilities become less significant. Critical sexual theory can drill into many fissures, enabling one to explore how disabled women's marital sexual aspects become absent referents, permitting us to forget a woman with disability is an independent entity or a normal human with similar needs and desires as the so-called able-bodied. For example, disabled women are deemed asexual. These women are also considered to be passive recipients of sexual activity, whereas a male partner is proactive, which is linked to the ideas of virility and manliness. These ideas as discourse are linked to gendered-sex issues that control women's bodies (Foucault, 1990). In addition, there are other social and cultural expectations that tend to cloak women's emotions from being actively revealed (Foucault, 1990).

While discussing critical sexual theory and disability, Foucault's (1990) biopower is equally important in an analysis of disability. As biopower is having power over other bodies, it has been used in relation to practices of public health, regulation of heredity, and risk regulation, among many other regulatory mechanisms often linked less directly to physical health. Foucault (1990) explored this phenomenon further in his lectures on biopower:

> By this I mean a number of phenomena that seem to me to be quite significant, namely, the set of mechanisms through which the basic biological features of the human species became the object of a political strategy, of a general strategy of power, or, in other words, how, starting from the 18th century, modern Western societies took on board the fundamental biological fact that humans are a species. This is what I have called biopower.
>
> (p. 129)

The idea of biopower questions the legitimacy of governmental institutions and political power, while defending individual power. It helps us understand disabled women and the political and social powers that oppress them. Foucault (1990) proposed that power is not something given, but rather is exercised. Biopower can be linked to sexuality. According to Foucault (1990), "sexuality must not be thought of as a kind of natural given which power tries to hold in check, or as an obscure domain which knowledge tries gradually uncover" (p. 105). It is instead:

> the name that can be given to a historical construct: not a furtive reality that is difficult to grasp, but a great surface network in which the stimulation of bodies, the intensification of pleasures, the incitement to discourse, the formation of special knowledge, the strengthening of controls and resistances, are linked to one another, in accordance with a few major strategies of knowledge and power.
>
> (Foucault, 1990, pp. 105–106)

In other words, sexuality is socially, culturally, and historically constructed. Foucault (1990) further stated:

> Thus, sex gratitude became an object of great suspicion; the general and disquieting meaning that pervades our conduct and our existence in spite of ourselves; the point of weakness where evil portents reach through to us; the fragment of darkness that we each carry within us: a general signification, a universal secret, an omnipresent cause, a fear that never ends.
>
> (p. 69)

The way in which sex has been discussed creates a hegemonic pressure, connecting it to the idea of morality versus immorality, good versus bad, and life versus death. Sex is deemed to be practiced through marriage. The laws and rules are interpreted, and sex is made private. This unseen power is imposed. In this regard, Foucault (1990) asserted:

> Power is essentially what dictates its law to sex. Which means first of all that sex is placed by power in a binary system: licit and illicit, permitted and forbidden. Secondly, power prescribes an order for sex that operates at the same time as a form of intelligibility: sex is to be deciphered on the basis of its relation to the law. And finally, power acts by laying down the rule. Power's hold on sex is maintained through language, or rather through the act of discourse that creates, from the very fact that it is articulated, a rule of law. It speaks, and that is the rule. The pure form of power resides in the function of the legislators; and its mode of action with regard to sex is of a *juridico* discursive character.
>
> (p. 83)

Power limits sexual freedom and sets barriers exerting the idea of appropriate versus inappropriate. As well as applying to the able-bodied, in the context of this study power applies to individuals who are disabled. As previously mentioned, disabled people are sometimes described as being either asexual or highly sexual. Therefore, when disabled people's sexual needs linked to marriage are discussed, they are ignored because disabled people are deemed to not have sexual desire or to be inappropriate, especially women. Historically, women's bodies are defined as *hysterical*, in other words, overly emotional and irrational. Foucault (1990) discussed the hysterization of women's bodies and how they are qualified and disqualified in different spheres of life and in social and familial contexts:

> A hysterization of women's bodies: A threefold process whereby the feminine body was analyzed – qualified and disqualified – as being thoroughly saturated with sexuality; whereby it was integrated into

the sphere of medical practices, by reason of pathology intrinsic to it; whereby, finally, it was placed in organic communication with the social body, the family space, and the life of the children; the mother, with her negative image of "nervous woman," constituted the most visible form of this hysterization.

(p. 104)

This clearly shows how sex is gendered, or how the biological becomes social. In relation to women, it becomes more of an issue of morality. Foucault (1990) discussed sexuality in the Victorian era, including how the natural spheres of male and females were stratified and decency was maintained. Sex was connected to morality and decency. A woman was either a whore or a mother, Mary the Mother of Christ or Mary Magdalene the prostitute. The purpose of sex was utilitarian, for procreation. The Foucauldian discourse on sex in a different context, however, informs Nepali religious and cultural perceptions of marriage and sex, in which to have sex before marriage is considered filthy, unhealthy, and immoral. Society looks down upon people who do so, especially women.

This talk of sex, in Foucault's (1990) terms, is "repressed to silence" (p. 105). In a culture where sex is considered taboo, society hardly recognizes the significance of sex in human lives other than as a means of reproduction, and when it is joined to a disability, sex is less important (Epstein, O'Flynn, & Telford, 2001; Raghavan & Vora, 2016). These ethos, thoughts, and discourses on sex pervade different institutions in a society where marital sexual lives of people with disabilities are repressed (Raghavan & Vora, 2016). Policies formulated to address the lives of the disabled turn out to be hegemonic due to the influence of these discourses, which tend to impose censorship and silence in their personal spheres of life.

When disability is viewed alongside gender sexuality (male versus female and sexual versus asexual), friction is created, as they are considered opposites. This is because, again, having a disability is viewed as being inherently asexual (Bernert, 2011; Cuthbert, 2017). This understanding of sexuality and disability is oppressive because it embodies society's standard heteronormative understanding of sexuality, which creates binary divisions between able and disabled, sexual and asexual (Cuthbert, 2017; Kim, 2011; Shuttleworth, 2007).

In this regard, Foucault's (1990) discourse on sexuality and the idea of disciplinary institutions can add to critical sexual theory, which can help not only understand how the disabled body is controlled, but also help explore the sexuality of the disabled, that is, the binary expression of sexual and asexual among the disabled. Disciplinary institutions impose limitations that disabled people might have experienced as a result of the "protective policies and programs" (Bernert, 2011, p. 131). Protective policies and programs rely on people viewing people with disabilities as asexual or incapable. Relying on protective policies and programs, agencies or organizations that have been working for people with disabilities deem what is appropriate and what is not, which imposes certain hegemonic power over people with disabilities. In the name of making best choices on behalf of people with disabilities, protective policies and programs control and, metaphorically speaking, tame the marginalized subject (Foucault, 1990). In the context of disciplinary institutions, rehabilitation focuses on adjustment, which fails to understand and incorporate the sexuality of people with disabilities (Foucault, 1990; Shuttleworth, 2007).

Critical sexual theory aims to look beyond the normative aspect of sexuality based on heteronormative society; it sees beyond the opportunities of employment and education and disabled-friendly infrastructure. Critical sexual theory can help include disabled people's voices regarding their marital and sex perceptions. Shuttleworth (2007) proposed that: "An academic and political alliance with sexual and gender minorities and their allies, one hopes, [will] lead to innovative approaches for tackling some of the difficult policy issues in sexual politics" (p. 4). This type of theoretical approach also helps gauge whether disability policies and agencies working for the disabled repress their sexuality. Thus, critical sexual theory in the study of disabled people's marriage and sexuality is a "critical interrogation of the salient social, cultural, representational, political, psychological, and emotional aspects that effectively constitute the sexual oppression of the disabled people" (Shuttleworth, 2007, p. 6). Furthermore, it can be a tool for the interrogation of oppressive structures that restrict the sexual lives of the disabled and can help bring their voices to policy makers.

Nepali and Indian women, in particular, are expected to conform to manufactured standards of beauty. The social standards for women's beauty are defined as physically normal. Critical sexual theory investigates how the normative standard of physical beauty disqualifies the sexual ability of disabled women. Shuttleworth (2007) suggested that if these women do not fit into a standardized conception of beauty, feelings of sexual inadequacy and low bodily self-esteem are internalized as "asexualness" (p. 5). Looking into how biopower controls the marginalized subject or how disciplinary institutions pervade the lives of disabled women in the context of the Global South may help one understand different social characteristics that marginalize women with disabilities and the power relationships, not only between men and women, but also among high-caste women and *dalit, adivasi,* and *janajati* women. Thus, to discuss the marital sex lives of the disabled, it is important to understand Foucauldian discourse – a discourse that is "a body of anonymous, historical rules, always determined in the time and space that have defined a given period, and for a given social, economic, geographical, or linguistic area, the conditions of operation of the enunciative function" (Foucault, 1969, p. 131). Understanding Foucauldian discourse helps understand biopower and how power is exercised in different and sometimes competing ways, some of which become fixed, hegemonic, and normative.

Foucault's (1990) biopower helps one understand if or how women with disabilities are controlled or oppressed through disciplinary discourses that have to do with gender and sex. For example, a woman may be socialized to believe that she should not talk loudly, not come out of the house often, or not talk to people so as to maintain decorum or follow the Laws of Manu (Ghimire, 2010; Olivelle, 2005). These rules of etiquette for women in society permit others to forget them as independent entities, and therefore, they are prone to be discriminated against. The social structure and disciplinary discourses imposed on women, as Foucault (1990) suggested, tame them as the marginalized subject. Analyzing narratives of women with disabilities in Nepal is particularly important for exploring the biopower that has oppressed their sex lives and for informing the lives of other women with disabilities in the context of both the Global South and the Western world. Since women with disabilities in Hindu nations intersect with gender and other social characteristics such as race, color, and ethnicity, it is crucial to discuss biopower to assess whether the discourse of sex, morality, and disciplines further marginalizes the bodies of women with disabilities.

The discourse on sex and gender in a South Asian context, as discussed in the book previously, ties into Foucault's (1990) work on the history of sexuality in the West, transforming the understanding of sexual, erotic, and aesthetic pleasure and gender relations (Gautam, 2017). Instead of acknowledging gender relationship only in terms of giving births to children, acknowledging the gender relationships in terms of pleasure and emotional relationship may help explore how biopower prevents women from their abilities from establishing relationships with their partners for pleasure. Foucault (1990) wrote: "The rallying point for the counter attack against the deployment of sexuality ought not to be sex desire, but bodies and pleasure" (p. 57). Foucault's perspective on the history of sexuality provides a better understanding of the notion of pleasure for "the contemporary debates on the history of sexuality, exotics, gender relations, and knowledge formation in different cultures" (Gautam, 2017, p. 21). This discussion brings with it a focus on the idea that sex and sexuality are intertwined to morality and immorality, sin and redemption, transgression and transformation, life and death, and so on (Foucault, 1990). The way these ideas are discussed in different cultures become discourse that either liberates or oppresses the society.

Critical sexual theory as a tool can help discover oppressions on women on their journey, leading them to marital and sexual emancipation by bringing their voices to the forefront. Giving women the opportunity to narrate the stories of their marital and sex lives may help them express their sexual desires, feelings, and sexuality (Shuttleworth, 2007). It may also help liberate them from the repression that causes frustration and anxiety. Freud and Strachey (1989) asserted that: "It is well known that temptations are merely increased by constant frustration, whereas an occasional satisfaction of them causes them to diminish, at least for the time being" (p. 87).

To break the stereotypes, taboos, and conservative practices in a society, critical sexual theory remains significant in the study of the marital and the gendered lives of women with disabilities. This remains significant not only in the lives of women with disabilities, but also in the lives of all humans. Critical sexual theory enables one to explore sex issues of the disabled beyond how people view disabled people as asexual. Shuttleworth (2007) proposed that: "A reworking and (re)deployment of the concept of sexual access beyond its current hegemonic biases might lead to insights into disabled people's sexual issues" (p. 4). The idea reinforces the significance of critical sexual theory as a tool for assessing how people conform to the standardization of gender and sex.

In relation to how disabled people conform to the standardization of sexuality, Grossman (2003) suggested that: "The notion of development tends to homogenize bodies and minds, sensations and emotions, with the description of one trajectory for all people within a given population" (p. 2). Grossman (2003) further wrote: "As a result, the sexual identity development trajectories of disabled people are disciplined with silence for their unwillingness (or inability) to conform to the standard" (p. 2). These ideas are relevant to the lives of disabled women in the Global South because this conformity to the standard of beauty and sexuality tends to disable their sexual ability.

Meekosha and Shuttleworth (2009) underscored the importance of critical theory in disability studies to look at things beyond a social model. They emphasized an explicit understanding of not only the social, economic, and political aspects, but also the psychological and emotional aspects of people with disabilities. This theory also helps critique disabling structures and assess conditions beyond the normalizing culture and standards of society. Meekosha and Shuttleworth (2009) also asserted:

> The defining feature of autonomy that interweaves throughout critical theory's history is its meaning as emancipation from hegemonic and hierarchical ideologies that structure personal consciousness, representations, social relations and practices in everyday life. Critical social thought is squarely at revealing the power relational dynamics within societies as manifested and reinforced via these seemingly innocuous means, at both the individual and the societal levels.
>
> (p. 53)

Meekosha and Shuttleworth (2009) emphasized the importance of autonomy, recognizing the social ideologies that shape a person's consciousness and identifying the true consciousness of people with disabilities. This recognition and identification help uncover alternative understandings of people with disabilities and society where they live in.

McCabe, Cummins, and Deeks (2000), Shuttleworth (2007), and Stevens (2008) discussed the importance of sex in the lives of people with disabilities. McCabe et al. (2000) emphasized that sex is "central to the lives of people" with disabilities (p. 115), as sex represents the emancipation of the individual and his or her right to achieve a better quality of life. Thus, this book examines disabled people discussing gender and the marital sex lives of women with disabilities, for example, drawing on the lives of five individuals from Nepal as a case study. To examine these narratives of disabled women, critical sexual theory and postcolonial studies have been used as a framework. To assist in understanding disability and the marital sex lives of women with disabilities, the next section provides a review of postcolonialism.

Postcolonialism

Postcolonialism is the academic study of the cultural legacy of colonialism and imperialism; this study focuses on the human consequences of controlling and exploiting colonized people and their lands (Said, 1979). It is a postmodern concept that looks at the world from the perspectives of colonized people. To understand the term *postcolonialism*, it is important to understand the relationship between the colonizers and the colonized. Many countries around the world were colonized, mostly by European powers, and many colonizers, such as the British, felt justified and morally obligated to teach and mentor people in these colonies who they thought were less civilized and childlike. Thus it was in this way that the colonizers exerted their power over the colonized (Brinkley, 2010; Said, 1979).

Postcolonialism emerged as a way of examining the relationship between the colonizers and the colonized. Postcolonialism can also be interpreted as the decolonization of the colonized. This implies, as Fraser (1985) proposed, that the key to an emancipatory outcome lies in the conception of decolonization. Decolonization is another aspect of critical theory that helps deconstruct the "social meanings of 'wo-man' and 'man,' 'femininity' and 'masculinity'; over the interpretation of women's needs; over the interpretation and social construction of women's bodies; and over the gender norms which shape the major institution-mediating social roles" (Fraser, 1985, p. 124). The idea of postcolonial studies overlaps with critical theory, especially with Foucault's (1990) concept of biopower, as it helps bring the narratives of the disabled, voices of the marginalized, and voices of the colonized into view.

Postcolonialism as a theoretical approach can help uncover the knowledge of the colonized (non-Europeans, or Easterners, in this study) from their own perspective (Said, 1979). If one deconstructs/debunks how the colonized is viewed by colonizers, one can understand the colonizers' hegemonic power over the colonized. The colonizers are the ones who preside over the colonized with their own perception and knowledge of the colonized. The knowledge of the colonizers over the colonized is an ideology, a false consciousness, which is hegemonic. Metaphorically speaking, postcolonialism in this study is used as a tool to bring the knowledge of the disabled to the so-called abled. With this knowledge, one can discover the knowledge or different ideologies of the disabled versus the abled. According to Marx and Engels (1848), an ideology is a false consciousness controlled by people in power. This kind of imposition creates a colonial discourse by creating binary divisions of appropriate and inappropriate, parent and children, student and teacher, direct support professional and disabled, and master and slave. The former becomes a colonist, and the latter becomes a colonial subject in colonial discourse.

The term *colonialism* emerged along with the Westerners' invasion on Easterners' land and property, taking control of the people and places, as well as their culture and knowledge (Brinkley, 2010; Said, 1979). The colonizers reaped benefits from what they deemed their colonies, and the colonized people became the subjects that the colonizers read and studied, understood and perceived from a perspective of dominance. In this regard, postcolonial studies aim in part to deconstruct the perception and social and political knowledge of meaning, the colonized used the language/words the colonizers used to the colonized, such as "uncivilized," "wild," "exotic," childlike and so on. Using the colonizers' words to the colonized, the colonized backfired on the colonizers (Dirar, 2007; Said, 1979). In postcolonialism, the social and cultural perspectives of the subaltern colonial subjects, including their creative resistance to the culture of the colonizer, reveal the binary opposition of us and them (Spivak, 2010). The colonizers or the colonists become *us*, and the colonial subjects or colonized become *them* (Dirar, 2007; Said, 1979; Spivak, 2010).

In the past, colonization was a physical encroachment on the territory of Third World countries and other non-Western countries (Said, 1979). Later, colonization took place for religious missionary, trade, and other business purposes. More recently, colonization has taken the form of ideological (e.g., education) and technological invasion. Similarly, the work of nongovernmental organizations (NGOs), international nongovernmental organizations (INGOs), and charity organizations to aid the needy in economically developing countries can be considered, directly or indirectly, to be another form of colonization or hegemony of powerful/rich nations over developing and poor countries (Foucault, 1990; Said, 1979).

Gilbert and Tompkins (1996) defined postcolonialism, explaining:

> Post-colonialism is, rather, an engagement with, and contestation of, colonialism's discourses, power structures, and social hierarchies. . . . A theory of post-colonialism must, then, respond to more than the merely chronological construction of post-independence, and to more than just the discursive experience of imperialism.
>
> (p. 120)

According to Said (1979), postcolonialism is the concept that cultural representations are generated with the "us and them" binary relation. Us and them are social constructs that are mutually constitutive and cannot exist independent of each other because each exists on account of and for the other. Notably, the West created the cultural concept of the East, which enabled the Europeans to suppress the people of the Middle East, Indian subcontinent, and Asia and prevent them from expressing and representing themselves as discrete peoples and cultures (Said, 1979). As Foucault (1994) argued, knowledge creates truth, and the truth creates power; thus, power and knowledge are inseparable. Said (1979) asserted that power and knowledge are the inseparable components of the intellectual binary relationship with which Occidentals claim knowledge of the Orient. The applied power of cultural knowledge allowed Europeans to rename and redefine non-Western peoples, places, and things to become imperial colonies and to then control these colonies (Said, 1979).

Spivak (1992) developed and applied term "epistemic violence" (p. 24) to describe how non-Western ways of perceiving the world were destroyed by the dominance of the Western ways of perceiving the world. According to the author, epistemic violence is related to *othering* people, which specifically relates to women, whereby the "subaltern" (Spivak, 1992, p. 24), such as a woman, must always be caught in translation, never allowed to truly express herself, because the colonial power's destruction of her culture that is pushed into social margins. The colonial power margins her non-Western ways of perceiving, understanding, and knowing the world. In establishing the postcolonial definition of the term *subaltern*, Spivak (1992) cautioned against assigning an overbroad connotation:

> *Subaltern* is not just a classy word for "oppressed," for The Other, for somebody who's not getting a piece of the pie. . . . In postcolonial terms, everything that has limited or no access to the cultural imperialism is subaltern – a space of difference. Now, who would say that's just the oppressed? The working class is oppressed. It's not *subaltern*. . . . Many people want to claim subalternity. They are the least interesting and the most dangerous. I mean, just by being a discriminated-against

minority on the university campus; they don't need the word "subaltern." They should see what the mechanics of the discrimination are. They're within the hegemonic discourse, wanting a piece of the pie, and not being allowed, so let them speak, use the hegemonic discourse. They should not call themselves subaltern.

(p. 26)

Spivak (1988) urged that "[t]he subaltern has no history and cannot speak" (p. 28).

According to Spivak, the subaltern is an oppressed group of people. It can be anyone belonging to the "lowest strata of the rural gentry, impoverished landlords, rich peasants and upper middle peasants all of whom belonged, ideally speaking, to the category of 'people' or 'subaltern classes'" (Spivak, 1988, p. 26). All who are oppressed cannot be subaltern, but all subaltern can be oppressed. The subaltern can be heterogeneous in its composition or demographic, and economically and socially uneven. A class, a group of people, or a person "dominant in one area could be dominated in another" (Spivak, 1988, p. 26).

Postcolonialism is a new way of challenging or deconstructing colonial domination. Loomba (2001) argued that postcolonialism is not a term that signifies the end of colonialism, but rather signifies new forms of contesting colonial domination and the legacies of colonialism. In this sense, it is about examining the relations of domination between and within nations and cultures and recognizing the historical roots of such practices within colonialism.

Relating this idea of postcolonialism to disability, there are many authors who have discussed disability in the context of postcolonialism. Shakespeare (2000) brought in postcolonial theorists, such as Edward Said (1979), to compare the disability experience to that of colonialism and imperialism. Discussing disability in light of postcolonialism helps identify the cultural, social, historical, and sexual aspects of disability and differences in the existing culture. In this light, the way the disabled are viewed is similar to the way the colonized are viewed: both are believed to need support, care, and mentorship without which they will be abandoned and uncivilized. Memmi (1991) observed:

> In the early twentieth century, residential institutions were often actually called "colonies." Still today, people who receive welfare or medical help may be taken over, their homes or bodies invaded. In return for help, they have to give up control over their lives. The colonialism incipient in the caring relationship can mean that the power to define the problem, let alone the way that the problem should be solved, is removed from the person and monopolized by the helper.

(p. 190)

Memmi (1991) elucidated that the help-receiver may be regarded as incapable, incompetent, and sometimes even genetically and morally inferior, similar to attitudes toward indigenous peoples in the former colonies. Some of those words Said (1979) also used to describe the life of the colonized, such as other, them, alien, uncivilized, and exotic, reflect on the lives of the disabled (Garland-Thomson, 1997). Sherry (2007) expressed that: "This metaphorical connection between disability and postcolonialism are so extensive that they cannot be fully summarized in one brief paper" (p. 16). We can apply this idea to many settings. For example, a disabled person as a patient becomes medically colonized under the medical gaze (Foucault, 1994).

Medical gaze and colonization of the body

Foucault (1994) coined the term *medical gaze* to denote the dehumanizing medical separation of the patient's body from the patient's person (p. 107). Foucault used the term describing the creation of a field of knowledge of the body. In the analysis of the body, power interests are mixed. In entering the field of knowledge, the human body also enters the field of power, becoming a possible target for manipulation (Foucault, 1994). The way that colonizers invade the lives of people and places and colonized them, when entering the body of the disabled, doctors as colonizers perceived, studied, and knew their body as medical colonizers. Through examination (gazing) of a body, a doctor deduces symptom, illness, and cause, therefore achieving understanding of the patient – hence, the doctor's medical gaze was believed to penetrate surface illusions in near-mystical discovery of hidden truth. To this day, medical doctors in the West are for some, placed on an almost mystical pedestal in society, much like the role Western colonizers cultivated in Eastern colonies.

4 Qualitative methodology

Research design and data collection

For this book and for my case studies about five individuals from Nepal, to collect written material such as disability-related policies, legal documents, and reports, I contacted NGOs and INGOs for women with disabilities and visited libraries in Nepal and government offices. These included the National Federation of Disabled, Nepal (https://www.nfdn.org.np/); the Nepal Society of the Disabled (http://www.nsd.org.np/); and the Disabled Women's Organization (http://www.ndwa.org.np/). These organizations provided me with their informational brochures and monthly journals and also referred me to additional online resources on their respective websites. Thus, the sources for this study included government documents, papers on disability policy published in newspapers and journals, and any archives related to disability policies, as well as autobiographies or (non)fictional by women with disabilities. Only secondary sources were used for this study; no interviews were conducted. Since the social, historical, and cultural experiences of women are different than men's experiences, their unique experiences are studied independently and not combined into one analysis (Thomas, 1999). This allowed me to understand how women express their gender differently than men in their literary works.

I read autobiographies, poetry, fiction, and nonfiction written by disabled Nepali women, as well as any published works based on the life stories of the select disabled women (see Table 4.1). I used narratives and stories from the disabled women's published poetry, novels, and autobiographies that were publicly available and coded them using NVivo. I noted the significance of autobiographies that should inform policy (Griffiths & Macleod, 2008). Griffiths and Macleod (2008) asserted that:

> The autobiographies of people marginalized for reasons of gender, race, disability and social class has much to offer to those decision makers. Finally, autobiographies may be relevant because of the way they help its audience reframe an issue, by making the familiar strange

Table 4.1 Types of textual analysis

Types of analysis	Meaning	Application in disability analysis
Thematic analysis	Themes/patterns are built to describe important main ideas	How are the stories of the disabled women's sexual lives similar, and how are they different? What major themes are addressed?
Structural analysis (Barthes, 1975)	Provides explanation and analysis for ideas such as abstract concepts	What is disability? What is sexuality? How are disability and sexuality viewed in different contexts?
	Signifiers and signified(s); forms and content	Are there other factors to determine the disabled women's understanding of their sexual lives?
Dialogic/ performance analysis	Ideographs, metaphors	Choice of words? How does the critical theory lens communicate with the symbols, metaphors, and so on? Which binary oppositions are represented in the story (narratives)?
Visual analysis		

and giving a different perspective on what was personally taken for granted. Autobiographies are more or less the subject of policy.

(p. 134)

After collecting select disabled women's narratives and the stories of their sex lives, I conducted the narrative analysis. With the help of narrative analysis, I explored the disabled women's conditions, interacting with the disabled women's lives through their stories, to understand their experiences. I coded the stories from literary works by finding the essence of the stories and created themes and subthemes gleaned from the narrative texts that I expected to arise, like common threads. Data analysis included descriptive coding of autobiographies, conceptually organizing categories based on properties or dimensions, and determining relatedness among categories to establish themes (Corbin & Strauss, 2008; Creswell, 2007). I categorized the responses/results from select narrative texts into main themes and subthemes using NVivo software. I categorized subthemes into positive and negative.

Why narrative method?

Many scholars of public policy and public administration have recommended the use of narratives and narrative analysis and how stories make sense to affect policy and policy making (Feldman et al., 2004; Griffiths & Macleod, 2008) by enabling participants in policy to "predict, empower, and even fashion change" (Boje, 1991, p. 124). Feldman et al. (2004) shared that "stories have been said to mediate reality and construct political space and are critical constitutive forces in politics and public policy making" (p. 147). Feldman et al. (2004) further asserted that: "Narratives are useful data because individuals often make sense of the world and their place in it through narrative form" (p. 148). By having disabled women telling their stories, one can grasp the political and cultural understanding of one being in a particular context. The analysis of the stories that people tell "provides insights not only into what is happening but also into the understanding of the people about why and how it is happening" (Feldman et al., 2004, p. 150). Narrative method serves critical theory by seeking the implicit and alternatives in the narratives, and discovers socially constructed reality, false consciousness, and false intersubjectivity.

Narrative analysis helps find the implicit in the narrative voices that helps expose alternative narratives that are useful in policy making. This creates a situation in which the meaning is made through binary opposition (Feldman et al., 2004; Miller, 2012). For example, in disability narratives, one can create an alternative meaning of what disability is from what it is not. Looking at the narrative within a postmodern context, it is a tool through which meaning is made through the practice of binary opposition. In this context of deconstruction, Abel and Sementelli (2005) explained that:

> All definitions are socially constructed, and reconstructed on a continuing basis, and variation in the meaning or the extension of a concept is a function of alternative evaluative perspectives. To understand the historically and culturally constructed meaning of something, deconstruction is employed, not to elucidate in the sense of attempting to grasp a unifying content or a theme, but to elucidate cultural biases, oppressive power relationships, and dominating epistemologies that secure patterns of advantage and disadvantage . . .
>
> (p. 16)

Examining cultural and social biases and oppressive power relationships, for example, between rich and poor or high caste and low caste, makes it possible to see underlying problems that policy narratives may fail to show. Thus, narrative analysis is crucial to guide policy making. Narrative analysis helps identify alternatives by discovering any gaps or mismatches between policy and lived experience. Narrative analysis helps find what the story implies through the discovery of how logic is made and how the syllogism is used (Feldman et al., 2004). Feldman et al. (2004)

described syllogism analysis as being used to "find logics that run across many different stories and to show how narratives construct archetypical characters that are simplistic representations of policy arguments" (p. 167).

Narratives are important policy tools because policy makers can draw conclusions about policy based on the "assumptions about characters that are implicit in the stories" (Feldman et al., 2004, p. 167). Narrative method values personal stories and enables marginalized voices to be considered in policy making. It is the reason why this study used narrative method to explore disabled women's narratives by entering into their autobiographical and other fictional and nonfictional works.

Griffiths and Macleod (2008) underscored the importance of autobiographical works to inform policy because the narrative inquiry helps one understand the "complexities of human behavior in the social context" (p. 123), as well as policy implementation. They also suggested that anecdotes can affect policy. In the context of educational policy: "[a]necdotes told to powerful people may change their minds about issues, where other sources of information and argument have not" (Griffiths & Macleod, 2008, p. 125), and they see much truth and validity in the narrative. In this regard, it seems crucial for policy makers to use the narratives of the disabled in policy making. Griffiths and Macleod (2008) suggested:

> There are some areas of study to which auto/biographical research can be seen as being particularly well suited. First, the experience of people at the margins, such as those whose lives intersect more than one dimension of difference such as race, class, gender, disability, or sexuality. Narrative research has been presented as a method for giving a stage to the voices of people who traditionally have had not been heard.
> (p. 137)

Critical theory and postcolonial studies play a synergistic role in identifying the oppression of the marginalized, the binary oppositions in us versus them, and can help bring the voices of the marginalized to light in policy. In this book, I chose disabled women's autobiographical works as part of the narrative inquiry because the study of autobiographies is important in uncovering implicit meanings. Again, Griffiths and Macleod (2008) pointed out that:

> Auto/biographical research may identify a problem that policy may be required to address, viewing things from a different perspective and thus identifying previously hidden issues – that are it can contribute to the setting of policy agenda. Auto/biography has a contribution to make to the refinement of policy, its evaluation and fine tuning. Finally,

because of the ability of auto/biography to capture the individual experience in a wider social context, and to represent complex and nuanced situations.

(p. 138)

Bruner (1991) stated that narratives are tools used to explore human experience and constructions of reality. Narrative reality is a story in which the narrator gives narrative form to experience (Gubrium & Holstein, 2009). The story gives a sense of what happened or what might happen. Lyotard (1984) suggested that in the postmodern condition, narratives create meaning in communicative and interactive settings. When the narratives are created, they are created to make sense for themselves, to make meaning of the self (Bamberg, 2011; McAdams, 1993). Many narratives include stories about individual lives, struggles, and experiences. Some narratives are in first person, some are in second person, and still others are in third person, reflecting on different experiences and perspectives.

Narrative analysis examines personal histories, biography, life history, and autobiography, as well as fiction, nonfiction, novels, and poetry, all of which contain the reflection of lived experiences and the quest for the self (Bamberg, 2003, 2011; Bamberg & Georgakopoulou, 2008). Thus, narrative has emerged as a new, but central, formatting device for the organization of self and identity. It helps define who we are, or who we think we are, through the realization of the stories we tell about ourselves (Randall, 1995). In this sense, the story becomes the data to be analyzed. Narrative inquiry seeks out the problem in the narratives through the stories that are weaved from the author's experiences, problems, and social and cultural issues and contexts (Chase, 2005). Thus, narrative method is useful for the human sciences (Riessman, 2008).

Czarniawska (2004) defined narrative method as a process that delayers grand narratives in social research. Providing an overview of the development of the narrative approach within the social sciences, Czarniawska (2004) emphasized the importance of narratives for qualitative researchers who want to explore new perspectives, characterizing narrative methods as a "naturalistic genre" (p. viiii) since they often reflect everyday life, or the "raw world as was lived and experienced by its subject" (p. viiii).

The history of narrative research dates back to hermeneutic studies of the Bible and up to the postmodern method that studies the underlying structure, while explaining the role of the narratives (Czarniawska, 2004; Lyotard, 1984). Narratives are everywhere; we live by narratives (Czarniawska, 2004). The narrative method employs hermeneutics, phenomenology, and ethnomethodology; it is an "alternative mode of knowing" (Czarniawska, 2004, p. 8) and a method of communicating, and it has importance in organizational theory, practice, and policy making. Czarniawska (2004) provided a clear overview of how stories are made, collected, provoked, interpreted, analyzed, deconstructed, put together, and set against or together with other stories. The narrative method has a definitive place in postmodern society (Lyotard, 1984).

The narrative method in qualitative research is a growing concern for students and scholars of social science. In the discussion of whether social science is a real science, narrative method plays a significant role (Czarniawska, 2004). Limiting research to the analysis of directly observational data cannot address the multiple social complexities in different cultural contexts with which researchers must contend. The narrative method helps researchers uncover the soft side that natural science has forgotten or left undisturbed (Czarniawska, 2004).

Some of the concepts that narrative method brings to qualitative research are explication, explanation, and exploration (Czarniawska, 2004). In qualitative research, a narrative method is important to understanding the lifeworld situations of a person, and how a person lives through or by narratives. Narrative method as an interpretative method; different forms of the narratives not only relate to organizational culture and storytelling but also aid in policy making (Czarniawska, 2004; Prasad, 2005; Yanow & Schwartz-Shea, 2014)

Narrative method as interpretive method

Interpretive method is an appropriate approach to address the questions asked in this study. The field of public administration is so eclectic that it has been enriched with a multiplicity of perspectives that range from social science to business administration, so it is in need of an interpretive method. Mailloux (1995) described interpretation as "reading, explicating, making sense" (p. 121). Interpretation involves the two "etymological senses – translation of a text and translation for an audience" (Mailloux, 1995, p. 121). This definition reinforces the idea that interpretation has much to do with multiple meanings of a text in multiple cultural contexts. Interpretation is hermeneutics that helps develop an understand of reality in multiple contexts (Prasad, 2005).

Hermeneutics can be discussed in relation to phenomenology. *Phenomenology* is the philosophical term for methods of investigating the meaning of experiences people have or reflecting on their own lived experiences (Prasad, 2005). Phenomenologists define reality as intangible, remaining in human consciousness in terms of how it is ordered, classified, structured, and interpreted (Prasad, 2005). Reality is socially constructed through the acts of interpretation. Thus, epistemology becomes more important than ontology, and interpretative method in qualitative research becomes more important than merely quantitative research, as this method aims to explore implicit meaning within narratives. It therefore necessitates an interpretative method embedded in historical and allegorical contexts (Mailloux, 1995). While interpreting, the interpreter's worldview, upbringing, and politics come into play (Mailloux, 1995). How to deal with these possible distractions or what theory is relevant for interpretation is a challenge of the interpretive method.

The questions posed in research can be ontological, epistemological, and methodological (Gray, 2003). There are many key reasons the interpretative method is relevant to modern research. This method helps uncover the implicit "complex, nuanced, and context-dependent social process" (Prasad, 2005, p. 6). Interpretation also helps discern the "underlying deep structure" (Prasad, 2005, p. 92) of a social reality. However, it has been criticized as dehumanizing because language is embedded in culture (Levi-Strauss, 1995). In addition, a hermeneutics lens, such as a narrative method, assists in the visibility of the implicit nature of a deep social structure.

Writing is a method of inquiry, a process of discovery (Richardson, 1994). There are many doubts and distrust that come into account in this method of inquiry in different contexts. Interpretive method helps identify hidden meanings in historical and cultural contexts and fill the gaps of doubt and distrust. Richardson (1994) observed that, "If a woman sees male violence as normal or a husband's right, then she is unlikely to see it as wife battering" (p. 518). This is a powerful metaphor to illustrate how the interpretative method plays a vital role in discerning behavior or actions when time, place, history, and culture are considered.

The interpretive method that lives side by side with the narrative method is important in modern research (Wilson, 2002). Wilson (2002) proposed that: "We live by narrative every day and every minute of our lives. . . . Narrative is the human way of working through a chaotic and unforgiving world" (p. 10). Judson (2009) suggested that merely reporting the facts might not enable the researcher to show the subjects as real humans until they turn the facts into narrative. Interpretive method provides leeway for analysis of narrative attached to culture and human evolution to help understand lived experiences.

Yanow and Schwartz-Shea (2014) explained that: "Interpretive researchers reject the assumption of the superiority of numerical data over other forms of data (e.g., sound, visual imagery, built space materials)" (p. xxi). This approach will help the researcher, or even workers in an organization, "interact with an object, understand it in a context of the work" (Schmidt, 1993, p. 6). The localized context, which includes local knowledge as well as data, is important to social science research. Facts and numbers alone cannot describe social reality.

Interpretation as hermeneutics in narrative analysis

Hermeneutics plays a significant role for "entering the lifeworld" (Prasad, 2005, p. 103) of the text, which could be an object, subject, word, or image, in the course of making sense. Hermeneutics shares a phenomenological view of the world (Institute of Applied Phenomenology, 2010). In the course of sensemaking, one goes through faith and suspicion. For example, reading policy statements in an organization or doing research in a context other than the researcher's (Prasad, 2005). Thus, hermeneutics requires the delayering of the text, and it enters into the subtext of the text to grasp the latent meaning and unmask the ideological mask that the researcher might not have considered (Prasad, 2005). As Goffman (1963) suggested, the subtext could be the "backstage," the text could be the "front stage," and the ideological mask could be the "masquerade" (p. 116). Stivers (1993) discussed the role of personal narrative to help gain an understanding of women's worlds (private spaces) in this study from their perspectives, which otherwise would never have been acknowledged in public space. Without their voices, there would be no public discourse that includes their perspective.

Narrative has various meanings and is used in various ways that relate to the story and its context (Riessman, 2008). Symbolic interactionism within the narrative is the process of sensemaking (Prasad, 2005). Sensemaking is an enactment, the process of reality construction of something that is already in there in itself, yet to be explored, such as the lives in a drama, which is an "extension of symbolic interactionism" (Prasad, 2005, p. 44), where the characters perform a reflection of their social realities in multiple ways (Weick, 1995). The metaphor, "theater of the mind," helps us understand making sense of the self (Goffman, 1963, p. 126). Language and interpretation guided by the culture and the context of the individual occur within the mind. This emphasizes the notion of sensemaking in everyday life and lived experiences, and how people make sense through language in everyday situations (Prasad, 2005).

Regarding interpretive research, Yanow and Schwartz-Shea (2014) described the role played by researchers' "*a priori* knowledge, and their research subjects' situatedness in a context, and the interactions between consciousness and the embodiments of meaning in the form of texts, objects, and acts" (p. i). In the sensemaking process, the "conceptual boxes" or the "categories of thought" (Yanow & Schwartz-Shea, 2014, p. 10) play a role in making sense of the world. In social research, a step closer to a shared truth can be made through narratives that involve symbolic interactionism, which helps bridge the gap between the author and the reader (Bochner & Ellis, 1995). Unlike the positivists' focus on quantitative research, it touches on the aspects that the positivists fail to see or ignore in not looking at other perspectives (Cooper, 2010; Huberman, & Saldaña, 2014).

Data analysis: narrative analysis

In this book, I have used Barthes' (1975) structural analysis and Riessman's (2008) interpretation of narrative analysis to conduct the data analyses of the select narratives in this study. Barthes' (1975) structural analysis describes a system of analysis based on functional units and discusses how meaning is made through the relationships of words and syntax, or its linguistic structure. There are three basic levels of the analytical system: functions, action, and narrative. Riessman's (2008) narrative analysis was based on four procedures: thematic analysis, structural analysis, dialogic/performance analysis, and visual analysis.

In terms of thematic analysis, I have relied on the images, metaphors, and ideographs of the narratives as discursive devices, and then categorized accounts or aspects of accounts that are being told. I began by collecting the narrative (narratives/life stories) from disabled women's fictional works and coded summary ideas. Relying on stories elicited from fictional and nonfictional works by the disabled, I built themes and related the stories to the central themes of negative or positive perceptions of disability, as well as other cultural contexts of disability.

Next, I revisited the initial coding and developed a list of categories, and finally, moved from categories to concepts. I also looked into different social, political, and cultural contexts in light of the discursive devices discussed previously in which the narratives are structured and determined what the language in the stories did on both textual and cultural levels (Riessman, 2008). Thematic analysis also helped identify common themes (Riessman, 2008).

I worked to find "abstract, complicating action, resolution . . . [and] the sequence of speech acts" (Riessman, 2008, p. 13) that thematic analysis might fail to discover. The analysis helped explore the ideas, such as the abstract concepts of sexuality, gender, and disability, and how they were viewed in different contexts. The analysis helped discover the underlying meaning from Barthes' (1975) structural analysis that emphasizes forms and content that Riessman's (2008) analysis might fail to incorporate.

Riessman's (2008) dialogic/performance analysis was useful in focusing on context and viewing the narratives as being multivoiced and co-constructed. Here, I discussed symbols, ideographs, and metaphors, and how they communicated with the reader. The choice of words and their denotative and connotative meanings might communicate the narrator's consciousness differently (Czarniawska, 2004; Riessman, 2008). Here, I applied critical theory and postcolonial studies to observe how binary oppositions were created or meaning was made (Abel & Sementelli, 2005; Adams, 2015; Fraser, 1985; Foucault, 1994; Spivak, 2010; Said, 1979).

At times, structural analysis and dialogic analysis served the researcher's purpose of using critical sexual theory. Table 4.1 displays the three different types of analysis – thematic, structural, and dialogic – used to assess the disabled women's narratives in this study. Visual analysis was omitted because there were not enough pictures or images to analyze. After the narrative analysis was conducted, the typology of the narratives of the disabled women and disability policies in Table 1.1 were tested.

For Barthes (1975), words (linguistic units) are important for the concepts they present. Barthes (1975) held that: "Narrative units are not linguistic units, but only connotative value" (p. 246). According to Barthes, there are many subsidiary notations, catalysts between two cardinal functions, and many things happen between the sentences, in the lapses and the meanings are made in the absences. Cardinal functions are those functions implicitly understood without being said, for example, the words "telephone call" will suggest other things, such as ringing, picking up, speaking, and putting down the phone, which are consecutive functions.

I saw the importance of the application of critical theory in studying the presence of the meaning in the absence, the things that happen between two cardinal functions, in bringing the unheard voices to view. Introducing critical theory to narrative analysis is the exploration of ways that communication is enhanced or limited by social, institutional, and structural parameters. For liberation from domination, critical theory leads to society's rational interpretation and transformation.

Other narrative units are called indices, which signify something that could be psychological, environmental, or cultural. They implicitly signify more than the word itself, providing locally relevant data in a particular context. Like "catalyses," which are "consecutive units" that help understand how language makes meaning, indices are marginally functional (Barthes, 1975, p. 248). Here is a good example:

> To drink a whiskey (in the hall of an airport) is an action that can pass off as a catalysis to the (cardinal) notation of waiting, but it is also, and at the same time, an index to a certain atmosphere (modernity, relaxation, reminiscence, etc.).
>
> (Barthes, 1975, p. 250)

In the narrative, the focus is from form to meaning, from articulation to integration, from units to the units of higher rank (Barthes, 1975).

A structural analysis of disability narratives, for example, focuses on the different symbolic nods, functional units, indices, or signifiers that work together within sentence structure. The symbolic nods in a sentence form attitudes or beliefs for or against people with disabilities or induce actions in other human agents; they form an individual's conception and reality of another, while deflecting other realities such as personhood in the other. A structural analysis of disability narratives facilitates an understanding of the complexity of women and disability, disability and sexuality as cultural/ discursive issues, and social and structural phenomena.

Narrative analysis is a methodological approach that allows us access to consciousness and meaning in its full context through interpretation (Czarniawska, 2004). Griffiths and Macleod (2008) stated that: "Narrative research has been presented a method for giving a stage to the voices of people who traditionally have had not been heard" (p. 137). Ewick and Silbey (1998) proposed that narratives have counterhegemonic potential to change society by giving traditionally ignored and marginalized voices the opportunity to speak, recognizing that knowledge production is political.

Narrative analysis also attempts to make sense of human experiences (Jefferson, 1978; Langellier, 1989, 1999; Robinson, 1981). The intention of narrative analysis is to extrapolate from narratives and better understand particular experiences. Narrative analysis is an interpretive discourse (Lyotard, 1984). It is an inquiry into how meaning is conferred onto experience, especially in narratives of personal experience about concrete life situations (Mandelbaum, 1989, 1993; Mishler, 1995, 2005). Narrative analysis in this study was used to make sense of people's stories, particularly narratives of lives, as in autobiographies, life writing, confessions, poetry, fiction, and other disclosures of identity (Weick, 1995).

The study of ideographs and metaphors in narratives helps unravel an alternative discourse, one of the major aspects of critical theory. Abel and Sementelli (2005) wrote that employing analytical techniques such as concept analysis, deconstruction, case studies, immanent critique, action research, hermeneutics, and "how cultural processes develop and maintain meanings, attitudes, values, beliefs, epistemologies, and power relationships among members and institutions of a society" (p. 66) are useful strategies of critical analysis. With narrative analysis, readers – without witnessing the conditions of disabled women – can envision their situations, problems, and difficulties. These stories of the disabled may call for awareness and action, to fight against social stigmatization and oppression, and to help improve the lives of disabled women. Czarniawska (2004) described narrative analysis as "a spoken or written text giving an account of an event/ action or series of events/actions, chronologically connected" (p. 17).

Narratives of the disabled

Narrative accounts of disabled people's life events feature emotions and authenticity that cannot be understood until they are shared. The richness of these emotions and the depth of authenticity are achieved through the acknowledgement of the narratives of the disabled by reaching out to the essence of their truthful lives. The narratives can aid in understanding the experience of disablement (Malhotra & Rowe, 2013). Narratives serve a purpose that a quantitative analysis fails to fulfill, especially in understanding the experience of the disabled and its stereotypes (Carbado & Gulati, 2003). "It brings a human face to the problem, thereby facilitating appreciation of legal barriers and discrimination experienced by marginalized groups including disabled" (Malhotra & Rowe, 2013, p. 10).

Narratives stress the specificity of experience of a story to convey its verisimilitude (Bruner, 1991). In a narrative research study on disability, Malhotra and Rowe (2013) argued that:

> Without narrative to provide the phenomenological understanding, it is likely as difficult for an able-bodied woman to appreciate what it is truly like to require assistance with toileting and bathing on a daily basis as it is for a man to appreciate the experience of child birth.
>
> (p. 11)

This underscores the importance of narrative accounts of disabled people in understanding the phenomenon of their lived experiences. The richness of experience that is collected from narratives is not possible through a statistical account of people who are marginalized and disabled (Mahoney, 1991).

5   Disabled women's narratives

Here, I examine the writings of five disabled women authors from Nepal: Radhika Dahal, Jhamak Ghimire, Sabitri Karki, Parijaat (Bishnu Kumari Waiba), and Mira Sahi. All of the authors are published; Waiwa and Ghimire are renowned authors. Some are blind, while others are physically challenged in other ways.

Some of the published narratives are in Nepali, and some are translated and published in English. The narratives that are not in English are quoted in Nepali *Devanagari* script and translated by the researcher. The select authors have shared their personal narratives through poems, novels, and autobiographies. These authors discuss sex, marriage, and disability. In reading the select works by these disabled Nepali women, the researcher examined what a woman's disabled body learns and gains from a society that sees the disabled body as asexual, malformed or deformed, and unfit for marriage and motherhood. In this chapter, the authors' fictional and nonfictional narratives are examined through the combined lens of critical sexual and postcolonial theories so as to assess whether the narratives reflect or challenge disability policies in Nepal.

Each author is introduced, followed by the analysis of her select narratives. The title of the narratives of each disabled woman, the themes the narratives are based on elicited via NVivo, and the themes the authors have in common are shown in Table 5.1.

Radhika Dahal

Born in the district of Sindhuli, Nepal, Dahal fell off a swing when she was a young child. She broke her backbone, causing a spinal injury. The injury rendered her a paraplegic. She could not continue her education as it was not easy to participate in the community due to her physical disability and the perceptions of others.

Later, she was locked up in the house. She never got married. When she was brought to the hospital for treatment, she was subjected to carelessness

Table 5.1 Narrative themes of selected writings of authors in this study

Author	Narrative	Main themes	Common themes
Radhika Dahal	*Pallo Ghar ki Budhi Fupu* (*An Old Woman Next Door*) (2014a), novel	Passion of love and youth	Love
	Pareliko Sandh (*On the Edge of Eyelashes*) (2010), collection of songs	Love	Gender and sex
		Marriage	Doctor experimentation
		Youth	Youth and adolescence
	Seto Kotbhitra Kalaa Man (*Black Hearts Inside White Jackets*) (2014b), nonfiction	Doctors and experiment	
		Sex and gender oppression	
Jhamak Ghimire	*A Street Child's Question to her Father* (Thapa, 2009), poem	Gender oppression	
	Jiwan Kada ki Phool (*A Flower in the Midst of Thorns*) (2010), autobiography	Gender and sex	
		Love and marriage	
		Doctor and shaman	
		Freedom	
		Youth and adolescence	
	Samaya-Bimba (*Time-Symbols*), (2014), nonfiction	Gender oppression	
		Love and youth	
Sabitri Karki	*Juneli Kabya* (*Full Moon*) (2009), collection of poems	Youth and adolescence	
	Samarpan (*Dedication*) (2007), collection of poems	Love and marriage	
		Love and nature	
	Utpidan (*Torture*) (2011), collection of poems	Love	
		Sex and gender oppression	
		Doctor and experiment	
Parijat (Bishnu Kumari Waiba)	"A Sick Lover's Letter to her Soldier" (Hutt, 2008), poem	Love and life	
	"In the Arms of Death" (Hutt, 2008), poem	Love and death	
	Mahatahin (*Absurdity*) (2013), novel	Love	
		Gender and sex	
	Shiris ko Phool (*The Blue Mimosa*) (1980), novel	Gender and sex	
		Unrequited love	
	"To Gopal Prasad Rimal" (Hutt, 2008), poem	Love	
Mira Sahi	*Atita ka Sushkeraharu* (*Whistles from the Past*) (2015a), collection of poems	Doctor and experiment	
	Pidha Bhitra ka Chhatpati (*A Stressful Struggle in Sorrow*) (2015b), collection of poems	Youth and adolescence	
		Love and motherhood	
		Sex and gender oppression	

and the reluctance of doctors to treat her seriously. The doctors paid more attention to the patients who were relatives of influential people, even if the patients' cases were not serious (Dahal, 2014a). Dahal (2014a) said it was because she was not well connected, did not belong to any minister's legacy, and was not financially rich. She said that perhaps her disability would not be that severe had she received prompt attention from the doctors on duty (Dahal, 2014a). She felt that they looked down at her and did not believe she deserved the same care as wealthier patients. Dahal's words fell on the doctors' deaf ears. Dahal believed she had a right to be treated because of the pain she felt in her body, but she was dismissed by the doctors attending to her. Her story exemplifies Foucault's (1994) medical gaze. Foucault (1994) stated

> The gaze that is turned upon it by those close to the sick person has the vital force of benevolence and the discretion of hope . . . no doubt there are sick persons who have no family, and others who are poor that they live "cooped up in attics."

> (p. 40)

In *Seto Kotbhitra Kalaa Man* (*Black Hearts Inside White Jackets*), Dahal (2014a) wrote about her experiences and of the comments she overheard from others wherever she went. These comments demonstrate how men perceived disabled women. "यी केटीहरुको जात जति टाठा बाठा र मै हुँ भने पनि, हामीजस्ता पुरुषको इशारामा गरुडको छायाँले नाग गुड्ल्किएझैँ लल्याकलुलुक हुन्छन" (These women, no matter how clever they think of themselves, surrender in front of men, like a snake rolls over itself in front of its God named Garud) (Dahal, 2014b, p. 69). In a Hindu myth, a snake is helpless in front of a god named Garud, and when the snake is compared to a woman, this underscores the belief that women are less capable in front of men or are poisonous evil characters likened to snakes. In her poetic narratives, Dahal wrote about her erotic feelings and desires, which men don't perceive in disabled women.

Dahal's poetic and conversational narratives deconstruct doubt as to whether women have feelings or desires as do men when one of the characters in her novel has misgivings about desire. Dahal (2014a) responded through a character, "अरे मुर्ख यस्तो त तँ जस्तो जवान पुरुषलाई मात्र होइन, बिष झरेकी नारीलाई पनि हुन्छ" (Oh, stupid, this happens not only to a young man like you, but also to an old woman who lost her youth) (p. 74). Dahal (2014a) further emphasized, "एउटा बगैचामा भर्खर फर्कदै गरेको सुन्दर फुलदेखे पछि, जवान पुरुष मात्र होइन, यहा बैंस झरेकी बुढी आईमाई पनि लालायित भएर लोभिन्छे" (When a young man sees a beautiful flower blooming in a garden, not only a young man, but also an old woman will be enticed by it) (p. 75).

Dahal's thoughts of each and every human are egalitarian. She does not see disabled people as asexual or as having fewer erotic feelings or desires, nor do they have to be deprived of what abled-bodied people can access. Dahal (2014b) wrote, "एउटा बगैचामा भर्खर फक्रदै गरेको सुन्दर फुल देखेपछि तिमी र मलाई मात्र होइन, यो संसारका जो कोहि मानिसंलाई यस्तै लाग्छ" (When a beautiful flower is blooming in a garden, not only you and I, but anyone who sees the flower will be impressed) (p. 87). Dahal (2014b) was extremely conscious of the significance of getting married, being a wife, and experiencing motherhood. She understood how important it was to be a mother in Nepali society. She saw how thankful women are to God when getting married, which reflects her own longing for marriage, although it is not explicitly stated in her conversational narratives. Underneath, Dahal (2014b) longed for marriage when she wrote, "श्रीमतीले आफ्नो छातीमा हात राखेर भनिन, 'धन्य भगवान तिमीले मेरो सिन्दुरको रक्षा गर्यौ'" (A wife puts her hand on her breast and says, "Thank God, you have protected my vermillion") (p. 92). Vermillion is a red powder that married women apply in a line right above their foreheads, and this makes them feel complete as married woman in Nepali society.

From another of Dahal's (2014a) novel's *Pallo Ghar ki Budhi Fupu* (*An Old Woman Next Door*), Dahal explored many of her curiosities through the character of an old woman. Perhaps, Dahal is, while looking into it critically, bringing her own unrequited desires into her writing. Dahal (2014b) wondered about the old woman's wants and desire and questioned: "के यिनको जवान मनमा उठेका अनगिन्ति रहर र चाहानाहरुलाई यो खोक्रो समाजको बेकामी आदर्शले संधै कैदी बनारै राख्न सक्यो त?" (Did the useless ideals of this hypocritical society continue making the old woman a prisoner of her body's wants and desires which cannot be fulfilled?) (p. 5). This reflects gender inequality and how women's freedom is controlled in a society that values patriarchal norms and standards.

In another book, *Pareliko Sandh* (*On the Edge of Eyelashes*) (2010), an anthology of Nepali songs, Dahal explored the love of her life, adolescence, the passion of love, and youthful life. These thoughts have seldom been explored in conversations with disabled women in a society where sex is deemed taboo and their desires and erotic feelings are generally deemed invalid. In each and every line, Dahal destroyed the myth of the asexuality of the disabled and showed how she celebrates her own desires, feelings, and emotions, which tend to remain absent referents in the lives of disabled women. Dahal wrote how her body is enriched with love. She wrote an evocative exploration of her wishes through a narrator other than herself.

Similarly, Dahal (2010) discovered her real wants in her narratives that Nepali society fails to understand. She showed her longing for marriage, a longing that society does not acknowledge or understand. Instead she is trapped in an environment in which people fail to perceive and study the wants, desires, and sexual feelings of the disabled.

From a critical sexual theory perspective, it helps to understand that Dahal's narratives explored the marginalized and subaltern aspects of her erotic feelings that are translated through her narratives. Dahal's narratives not only voiced her desires and feelings that are suppressed in a gendered society, but also deconstructed human perceptions of the disabled. Thus, the narratives would be useful in informing disability policies.

Jhamak Ghimire

Jhamak Kumari Ghimire was born in Dhankuta, Nepal. She suffers from cerebral palsy. She does not have control of her arms or her speech and does not have free bodily movement.

Sex and gender discrimination are apparent in her autobiographical narratives. Ghimire (2010) questioned: "What was her fault to have been born as a girl child? You had in fact wanted a son who would open the path of heaven for you" (p. 6). In Nepali culture, a son has to perform special ceremonial rites at the death of his parents, making the path to heaven clear after their death. This reflection encompasses the power of religion in the lives of people and the preference of sons over daughters in Nepali society. In a sense, a daughter is already disabled regardless of whether she is physically disabled because a daughter is unable to perform funeral rites. Without these religious rituals that only a son can perform, it is believed that parents who die will not have peace in paradise. This reflects how the inability of a woman to bear a son deprives her of personhood.

In a gendered and sexed society, Ghimire (2010) wrote how her father treated her badly. Ghimire's (2010) narratives speak about people's attitudes toward women with disabilities in a context in which patriarchal culture is dominant and people often view the demise of the disabled as the only solution to the challenges they cope with. Like Parijat, Ghimire (2010) hated how people sympathize with her disability as death, an ultimate option, and she abhorred the human cruelty of viewing disabled people as worthy of death.

Ghimire's (2010) voice against patriarchal society questioned: "Why did you damage me/on a corner of the street? Why did you fill my mind with gunpowder? Its transformation will leave your society and you poisoned" (p. 76). Ghimire compared herself to a street child, abandoned and forlorn, and questioned her father who stood for the patriarchal ethos in "A Street Child's Question to her Father" (Thapa, 2009). Ghimire resisted patriarchal cultural norms through her autobiographical narratives, railing at patriarchal society, a society that prefers sons to daughters. She wrote that males are to be blamed because they cannot choose what gender they implant in a woman's womb; a woman is like the earth that will reap what has been sown. She questioned why society believes the opposite. She reflected not only on her lived experience but also explored how gendered society further disables women's already disabled bodies. She questioned the deeply rooted gender/sex dichotomy in Nepali society, challenging the ancient, deep-seated male chauvinistic society, its social understanding, and cultural stereotypes.

Similarly, Ghimire (2010) underscored the necessity of sex, physical desire, and love, which are considered irrelevant to the lives of women with disabilities. She felt her body, her growth, and her sexuality when she looked at herself in the mirror. She enjoyed the erotic feelings within her, the feelings that society thinks are absent in the body of disabled women, a sign of moral decay, or a matter of taboo. Looking in the mirror, she wrote that when she looked at her vagina, she became amazed and overjoyed. Her vagina became a powerful metaphor and topic of discourse, referring to *The Vagina Monologues* (Ensler, 2001). She saw her vagina as a source of inspiration and joy, her beauty, and her life. She experienced her menstruation as a normal cycle of life in her body, but society put her away, saying that she was impure. She valued the significance of sex and asked people to respect it.

The "ideology of ability" that "determines the value of some sexual practices and ideas" over disabled people (Siebers, 2010, p. 136) does not allow one to think beyond the ideology box, but Ghimire (2010) brought to light what so-called able-bodied people tend to ignore in disabled bodies. Ghimire (2010) deconstructed the able-bodied idea of sex. Siebers (2010) observed that:

> The idea of sex life is ablest, containing a discriminatory preference for ability over disability. . . . One of the chief stereotypes oppressing disabled people is the myth that they do not experience sexual feelings or they do not have or want to have sex – in short, that they do not have a sexual culture.
>
> (p. 138)

Ghimire (2010) discussed her sex life, growth, and beauty by dismantling sex culture in the ablest society that determines how sex is viewed in the lives of women with disabilities, other than how disabled women themselves view sex and marriage. Ghimire (2010) realized what Siebers (2010) proposed about sexuality as a major part of a person's identity, that sexual liberation is good in itself, and that sexual expression is a civil right crucial to human happiness. This realization is evident when she described herself, her beauty, and the growth of her breasts in her autobiography. Siebers (2010) observed:

> First, thinking about disabled sexuality broadens the definition of sexual behavior. Second, the sexual experiences of disabled people expose with great clarity both the fragile separation between the private and public spheres as well as the role played by this separation in the history of regulating sex. Third, co-thinking sex and disability reveals unacknowledged assumptions about the ability to have sex and how the ideology of ability determines the value of some sexual practices and ideas over others. Finally, the sexual history of disabled people makes it possible to theorize patterns of sexual abuse and victimization faced by other sexual minorities.
>
> (pp. 136–137)

Ghimire (2010) underscored a dilemma regarding the private and public life of a disabled woman. She was not afraid to discuss sex and genitalia that the able-bodied devalue as abnormal and asexual. The narratives bring her most private into public. She wrote that she had lost her shame because she could not cover her shame by herself. She needed someone to fix everything for her. As she grew, she became aware of it. She did not let others get any enjoyment as they hurled pebbles, attacking her private parts. Defining her beauty and sexuality, she narrated that when society does not credit one with the value of a potential human, shame emerges, and sexuality remains distant. Thus, she addressed privacy by her narrative that reflects how people considered her asexual and abnormal.

Ghimire's (2010) narrative challenged the stereotype that disabled people do not have or want to have sex and do not have a sexual culture. She broke the normative assumption about a sex life, love, and emotions. She explored her body and its growth, and her sexual life. Her narratives about her own body and sexuality help one explore disabled women's sexual identity.

Ghimire (2010) explored the interference of people with her personal and sexual life as well. She mentioned the difficulty of having privacy from public view and how the able-bodied show their voyeuristic attitudes toward people like herself. Ghimire's (2010) narrative on sex and shamans reflected the gaze upon the disabled body as Foucault (1994) would discuss in his medical discourse. According to Foucault (1994), medical gazing involves the observation of physical symptoms and employing knowledge so as to come up with conclusions about a patient's body. Under the medical gaze, a person's structural body and its functional idiosyncrasies are supervised by physicians. The gaze asserts a cognitive relativity, such that the facts about the body are dependent upon the physician's medical gaze, including the physician's sensations, perceptions, and experiences. Though subjective by definition, the medical gaze also offers the physician an understanding of medical knowledge and a foundation for his judgments, so that his knowledge and observation of the body may be made useful. The diagnosis is based on the doctor's knowledge without the patient's perspective. The doctor's knowledge thus encroaches or interferes with the patient's body.

This idea is related to what Ghimire (2010) said about her body being watched and gazed at by medical doctors and shamans. She narrated the story of her disabled body upon which many shamans and doctors experimented to correct her cerebral palsy. She shared that her body was taken to shamans and witch doctors, but they could not fix her. When she was brought to the doctors, they simply said that her brain was damaged.

She wrote that looking at physically different people becomes a spectacle to entertain the viewers. Not only shamans, but also foreign doctors, tried to heal her body and make her normal. Ghimire's body became a colonized territory, an object, through the medical gaze; a ground on which people make discourse and interpret and create their own truth (Foucault, 1994; Said, 1979). She compared people around her looking at her body with people watching a strange bird in a cage, and like how colonizers perceive the colonized (Said, 1979). The relationship between the abled and the disabled is similar to how colonizers invade the territory of the colonized and think of civilizing them: people talking, guessing, and reading the sexuality or the issue of sex and marriage of the disabled in front of the disabled, which is no more than colonizing the disabled body.

From a postcolonial theory perspective, Ghimire (2010) showed how her body is viewed, defined, and colonized from able-bodied viewers or, metaphorically speaking, colonizers. The rientalization of the disabled body of women has worsened their condition. Ghimire's narratives challenge how nondisabled people colonize women's bodies and control how the disabled should be viewed. She brought the sexist culture that defined an able body into light and challenged the idea that culture is lodged in a healthy body and mind that only the able body can participate in.

Ghimire (2010) also explored how society indoctrinates superstitious cultural beliefs into children's minds, rendering them unable to overcome social prejudices related to gender and sex, sexuality, and marriage. This reflects how her sex as a female is gendered, oppressed, and invaded like colonizers entering the territory of the colonized. From a critical sexual theory perspective, Ghimire (2010) revealed her sex life, feelings, and emotions, as well as her own perception of sexuality and bodily growth through her vaginal discourse. Otherwise, they would remain absent referents that are related to disabled women's sex, marriage, and sexuality, and would have never been discussed. They would have been remained marginalized and colonized.

A cultural understanding of a particular context is key to exploring absent referents (Adams, 2015). Ghimire's (2010) conception of beauty deconstructed the existing beautiful versus ugly discourse in her culture to which social stigmas are attached. The social stigmas pass judgments upon disabled people, and the judgment fails to recognize the absent referents (Adams, 2015). They remain absent referents because people often avoid these topics in relation to the disabled body, but these absent referents become apparent in Ghimire's (2010) narratives.

Siebers (2010) proposed that the ideology of ability does not permit the idea that the disabled are sexual, or have legitimate feelings about beauty, health, and eroticism. When it comes to the love, marriage, and sexuality of the disabled, they remain invisible and ignored. However, one can see the importance of these things in the lives of the disabled. This reflects on how sexual discourse is created (Foucault, 1990). Sex in the lives of disabled women becoming a matter of taboo or moral decay does not allow people to think critically and explore absent referents, and disabled women have to live within the colonized territory of how they are defined or studied. However, Ghimire (2010) critically illuminated the absent referents by asking why the society in which she lives prefers males. Prejudiced perceptions of disabled people cloak the absent referents and bolster the ideology of ability and biopower (Adams, 2015; Foucault, 1990, Siebers, 2010).

Ghimire (2010, 2014) challenged the biased ideas in her patriarchal society to fight for the freedom of life. Her narratives disclosed the gap between what disabled women think of themselves and what people in general want for/how they view disabled people. One can hear Ghimire's voices in the gendered, sexist society through her narratives and reflect on many things that would otherwise have been missed, such as her own view of her body and her lived experiences.

Sabitri Karki

Karki was born in Bhaktapur, Nepal, circa 1970. She lost her sight when she turned 2 years old (Karki, 2007). She suffered from poverty and the stigma that went with being a disabled woman. Although her last name Karki is not of a lower caste, her writings suggest she that seems to have lived a lower-caste status, perhaps due to being a disabled woman. She has published a half dozen fictional works, mostly poetry.

After her father married another woman, her days of struggle began, but she survived it and achieved some success (Karki, 2007). Her husband is also blind, and they have two sons. Karki and her husband are both teachers at different schools in the same area. Their sons go to college and also help their parents with daily chores. Karki (2007, 2009, 2011) published many works after she finished her master's degree in Nepali literature. Although it was challenging for her to pursue her graduate degree, she completed her studies by successfully managing the difficulties she encountered. She observes, studies, and understands letters, words, or objects by touching them. Karki (2011) stated that she is able to impart quality education, but society's perception of her is that she is very feeble due to her disability. Most of her narratives are filled with discussions of the poverty in which she lived, the difficulties that she had to endure due to her disability, and people's perceptions of her disabled body. According to Karki (2011), to be a disabled woman in Nepali society is worse than being a disabled man. However, even if the facilities are not abundant, she is proud to have some accommodations for blind people, such as braillewriters and accessible computers.

Karki's (2007, 2009, 2011) narratives reflect the subaltern or marginalized position of women in the society in which she is living. The narratives reflect Karki's own conditions and experiences. This shows how, in general, menial jobs are assigned to women and that is why a women's name does not carry with it a good reputation. People pay attention to a woman when she is young, energetic, can work without a rest, and can please everyone, but she will be forsaken when she fails to have those qualities. Karki (2009, 2011) wrote satirically at times, claiming that she, as a woman, is a machine, so she does not need any rest. She also vented her frustration about the people of her own class, meaning women themselves are jealous of women, which shows the lack of unity among women and women's reliance on men. These ideas mirror what Spivak (1988, 2010) proposed about marginalized people.

People view disability as a lack that makes one incapable of receiving love and warmth, which are deemed to be consumed only by the able-bodied. However, Karki's poetic narratives dismantle the essentialist narratives that never allow one to recognize those qualities in disabled women. Karki (2009) talked about her own disability and explored how people cannot not hear about her fertile life as she explores her own wishes and desire to be a mother and be a married woman in her poem entitled "Disability." Thus, Karki (2007) worried if her desire for love would wither. She wrote, "प्रीतिको अङ्कुर यो नओईलाई सुक्न थाल्यो" (The seed of my love is almost going to die without being planted) (p. 15).

Besides the questions of being rejected and ignored as a woman in a patriarchal society, Karki (2007) expressed her desire for love and life relentlessly in her poetic narratives. She evoked her feelings that nature outside brings into her life romantically. She found everything complete, perfect, and full of life in a context in which people find disability a curse. She wrote how her body finds herself with nature. In her narratives, the narrator compares herself with nature, but her disability is not viewed by people in her society as something as wonderful as the coming of spring. More than that, Karki's narratives reiterate the longing for love and desires. She believes that not being able to see with the natural eye does not mean losing the desire for love, but rather the love and desires are even more deeply rooted because, she says, she sees things with a spiritual eye (Karki, 2007, 2009).

As with many disabled women's experiences with doctors, Karki (2009) also discussed her experiences. She described how doctors seemed to be reluctant to treat her at the hospital. This aligns with the discourse regarding how patients/disabled people in this context are simply ignored or abandoned, and why doctors fail to pay attention to what such patients need. Again, this relates to the discussion of the medical gaze, which is important to understanding the lives of disabled people when reflecting on their conditions in relation to existing disability policies.

Parijat (Bishnu Kumari Waiba)

Bishnu Kumari Waiba, also known as Parijat, was born in April 1937 in Darjeeling, India, into a Lama family. She was given the name Chheku Dolma, which would immediately be recognized by Nepali Brahmins as Lama, an extremely low caste bordering on being an untouchable. Later, she changed it to Parijat, meaning night-flowering fragrant jasmine flower, the flower everyone would like to touch. From birth, Parijat was physically incapacitated and became sick easily. When she turned 13 years old, she suffered paralysis that left her with a lifelong weakness. Parijat could not move around easily due to her physical disability and family restrictions (Prasai, 2010). Parijat felt her home was like a prison. Thus, she was held captive by her own body (Prasai, 2010). Parijat was thus introspective from her early childhood.

Parijat's mother died when she was young, denying her a mother's love and care. Her father was authoritative and restricted her from various ordinary activities, including leaving the house on her own (Prasai 2010). Parijat's father, a homeopathic doctor, treated her unsympathetically, refusing to grant her the freedom to live as she liked. Sometimes Parijat left home without getting her father's permission, which was against the traditional duty of a daughter. Prasai (2010) wrote that Parijat's father's authoritative and restrictive actions helped her fuel a revolutionary spirit against patriarchy, which manifested itself in behaviors such as smoking marijuana, which was deemed to be consumed only by men (Prasai, 2010). Smoking marijuana by a woman was and is still considered highly deviant, immoral, and against social norms and values. This suggests Parijat's defiance of her father's restrictions in patriarchal society. Despite the obstacles that her father, her society, and life put in her way, Parijat was able to overcome them and live as she chose, not how society anticipated her to live (Prasai, 2010).

As she got older, her health deteriorated, and she found herself suffering from a variety of illnesses. Later, she suffered from ulcers compounded by heavy drinking. Finally, she died on the April 16, 1992. She smoked, she drank, and she never got married. Smoking, drinking, and remaining unmarried were considered unusual in the life of a woman in Nepalese society. Hutt (2008) wrote, "She is unmarried and childless, a status that is not usual for a woman in Nepalese society" (p. 111).

Most of Parijat's narratives sprung "from her physical condition and from a profound atheism and moral despair" (Hutt, 2008, p. 113). "The themes and philosophical outlook of her poems, novels, and stories are influenced by her Marxist and feminist views and her own personal circumstances (Hutt, 2008, p. 111). This helps the reader analyze her narratives critically.

In her poem entitled "In the Arms of Death" (Hutt, 2008), Parijat expressed the outward appearance of an immobile body. The poem implicitly explains how her disabled body could be a barrier between her and other people because people ignored her as a person and focused on her disability. She emphasized that she is more than just what people see with the naked eye. The death imagery she used in her poetic narrative underscored her disability; her body cannot move as freely as a normal body does. She compared the bed to the tomb, and she called herself an "undying ghost" (Hutt, 2008, p. 117). The knowledge of her embodiment helps one understand the disabled body from the disabled's perspective. Parijat displayed her willingness to welcome death and celebrate her disabled body, which does not hope for or invite any sympathies from others.

Parijat deconstructed the notion of disabled people being viewed with sympathy. Sympathies that people pour into disabled bodies further exacerbate the conditions of the disabled as human sympathy fails to acknowledge the ability of the disabled. From a postcolonial perspective, Parijat's understanding of sympathy was that it fails to acknowledge the perspectives of the disabled in a particular culture and geopolitical context; rather, it reinforces the perspectives of the outsider regarding the disabled body, which is perceived, studied, and understood and, therefore, objectified by the so-called able-bodied. Viewing disabled people with sympathy creates a relationship of colonizers (nondisabled) and colonized (disabled). A critical theory lens helps one explore the gap in the discourse of colonizers and the colonized, which tends to remain invisible when the disabled body is viewed merely sympathetically. The subaltern, the colonized, or disabled in this context cannot speak (Spivak, 1988, 2010). This relationship between the one who is a sympathizer and the one who is sympathized exhibits binary oppositions. However, Parijat as disabled, understood the lapses in the understanding of the lives of the disabled when they are viewed solely with sympathies.

Parijat differentiates sympathies from love and intimacy. Although people might have sympathized with her out of love, her narratives expressed the lack of love and intimacy she received from her family, and she saw death not as something to be feared, but as something natural. At times, she expressed her love for life, unrequited emotions, and lack of motherhood, which was explored in the poem, "To Gopal Prasad Rimal" (Hutt, 2008). Parijat expressed that she cannot give the "ideals of motherhood" (Hutt, 2008, p. 114), which is an element that authenticates women's gender and sexual identity in Nepali society. However, she became critical of this notion of motherhood. The way motherhood is defined or studied in the body of the disabled does not reflect the reality of how motherhood is defined by the disabled body. It is not only linked to the idea of marriage and childbearing, but also is connected to ideas beyond the confinement of marriage. Parijat resisted the confines of her disabilities and mentioned revolutionary figures in her poems to symbolize her fight for freedom and emancipation, such as Buddha, Lenin, and Gandhi, who all took extraordinary routes to change societies.

In one of her most powerful novels, *Shiris ko Phool* (*The Blue Mimosa*), Parijat (1980) elevated the position of the female with disability higher than the able-bodied man. For example, Suyog, a male character in the novel, fails to meet, converse, and argue with the female character named Bari. Bari, who is physically handicapped, teases him to get married.

In another novel, *Mahatahin* (*Absurdity*), Parijat's (2013) narratives make the reader wonder about the narrator's sexuality, unfulfilled desires, and dreams. At times, the narrator (it is not clear whether a male or a female) says in Nepali, "उसको नाङ्गो पाखुराको चिसो मेरो आङ्गभरि सल्कदै थियो करेन्ट जस्तै" (His naked arms' chilliness was circulating through my body like an electric current) (Parijat, 2013, p. 5). The first-person narrator of the novel wonders about marriage, and the description is filled with sexual overtones and other desires. The narrator says: "बिबाह हुनु, मात्र एउटी स्वास्नी उपलब्ध हुनु थियो मेरा निम्ति अरु महत्त्वकाङ्क्षाहरु म मा केहि थिएन" (The purpose of marriage was just to find a wife for me. Besides that, I had no other ambitions at all) (Parijat, 2013, p. 10). This shows the narrator's desire for sex along with marriage, which deconstructs the concept of how the disabled body is viewed as asexual.

At times, the narrator imagines jealousy and sexual gratifications with another character named Shiya and that explodes in his or her imagination in this way: "सायद शिया आफ्ना फलामका खावाँजस्ता तिघ्रा नङ्गयाएर सुतेकी होलि र उ, कुन्नि को हो मलाई थाहा छैन, यसको मनपरी उपभोग गरेर बसेको होला" (Perhaps Shiya must have been sleeping with her pillar like thighs unzipped and I am not sure if there must be someone consuming her) (Parijat, 2013, p. 30). The narrator seems to be imagining the absurdity of life without sex as the narrator says this:

आफ्नु अस्तित्वलाई नै गिजोल्न इच्छा भईरहेको मलाई, यसो भन्, आफैलाई मार्न इच्छा लागिरहेको मलाई आवेसले पनि सास निभ्ने गरि घांटी अन्ठ्याईरहेको थियो, सम्झे यहि बेलुन संग एकपल्ट निर्लज्ज ब्यबहार किन नगरौ, किन यसैलाई नै आज अङ्गालोमा कसेर नहेरौ? खोई कहाँ छन् यसका इन्द्रियहरु? किन म यसलाईनै आज बलात्कार नगरुँ? (As I am going to misbehave with my own existence, or say, as I am going to kill myself, why should I not misbehave with the balloon I have? Why should I not hug it tightly? Why as there are no pictures or images to discuss should I not rape it?).

(Parijat, 2013, p. 32)

The narrator talks about him- or herself and sexuality saying, "बिद्रोहको लागि त म साञ्चै यौटा नपुङ्गसक थिएँ" (I was actually a gay for the sake of freedom) (Parijat, 2013, p. 43). These narratives from Parijat show sexual prowess in a context in which disabled people are deemed to be asexual and therefore unfit for marriage.

In "A Sick Lover's Letter to Her Soldier," (Hutt, 2008, p. 114), Parijat's body became a metaphor for the flower, a natural blossom that passes through many seasons and obstacles. Regarding sex and love, Parijat thought of them as a necessity and a natural process. According to Parijat, to have sex is easier than to love someone, and she expressed her unfulfilled physical desire for her first love because of her lower social status (Prasai, 2010). It was difficult for her to express her sexual or marital desire explicitly because she was a disable woman and from a lower-caste Tamang family.

From a critical sexual theory perspective, Parijat's narratives expressed her sexual liberation and self-determination despite how Nepali society views the disabled as unable, asexual, and abnormal. In this context, sexual liberation of the disabled and their self-determination become absent referents (Adams, 2015). Parijat's (Hutt, 2008) poetic narratives explored her own disabled body, which is unlike how Nepali society views it, and unlike what male bodies or nondisabled bodies have set as norms. For example, in her poetic narratives, Parijat expressed her love, freedom, desire, and the beauty of body, although her own physical body is incapable of moving freely. Parijat's narratives dealt with beauty, sex, love, sexuality, and growth, which are rarely considered in the lives of disabled women. In her narratives, love, sex, and marriage become absent referents that need to be explored to assess whether disability policies take them into account to recognize the abilities of disabled women.

From a postcolonial theory perspective, Parijat decolonized the perception of her body. Parijat proved the falsity of how people define, read, study, and colonize her body. Her fictional narratives deconstructed the Orientalization of her body, presenting her disabled characters in her fictional works as empowered. Orientalism is Said's (1979) concept regarding patronizing representations of the East, including the people and the societies who inhabit Asia and the Middle East.

In her narratives, Parijat (1980, 2013) implicitly asked who can say that the disabled body does not have feelings, emotions, and the desire to love and be loved (Hutt, 2008). The narratives echo desires and emotions of disabled women that people in general fail to see. So-called able-bodied people look upon the disabled body as crippled without desire for love and sex. Parijat's narratives define her disabled body not only as flesh but also as a location for love, emotions, and other desires of the flesh. Parijat defined love as the "union of bodies" that rises like a phoenix (Hutt, 2008, p. 115). Using an allusion to the mythological bird that is forever reborn from its own ashes, Parijat displayed the stamina of disabled women who otherwise are deemed to be languishing in the ashes of their lives. Parijat raised disabled women's voices, the voices of love, sex, and marriage of the disabled, which have become absent referents and are hardly discussed as key psychological and emotional aspects of disabled people's lives.

Parijat's (1980, 2013) fictional narratives are very revealing and outrageous; they break Nepali taboos by bringing out her voice (Hutt, 2008). Parijat's narratives destabilize the colonized perception of the disabled body and invite one to look into other psychological and emotional aspects of the disabled on their own terms. This shows that disabled women have not only explored the challenges they have faced due to their disabilities but also challenged the notion that disabled women are incapable and unfit for sex and marriage. These narratives have helped reflect on disability policies to explore the real issues disabled women are facing and their understanding of disability, which would further help support women with disabilities. While the policies seem to deny the ability of the disabled to engage in marital and sexual relationships, Parijat's narratives show her liberation from women's traditional roles by letting her desire for love and marriage go beyond the boundaries of her body as she fights against social stigmatizations and superstitious norms and values toward disabled people.

Mina Sahi

Born in the Dailekh district of Nepal in 1981, Sahi (2015a) is the youngest daughter of her parents. Her first publication is an anthology of Nepali poetry titled *Pidha Bhitra ka Chhatpati* (*A Stressful Struggle in Sorrow*) (Sahi, 2015b). Her second publication is *Atita ka Sushkeraharu* (*Whistles from the Past*) (Sahi, 2015a). Despite being born blind, she obtained her master's degree in Nepali literature. Most of her poems explore her experiences of how she suffered at the hands of able-bodied people. Sahi speaks up against people's attitudes and rejects perceptions of the disabled body. She is aware that women's disability is worse than men's as the culture prefers sons to daughters. She wrote how pathetic it is to be born as a daughter, and also, disabled.

One of her poems describes how a doctor used disabled people for experimentation. Like Foucault's (1994) medical gaze, in her narratives, Sahi (2015a) wrote that the body of the disabled becomes the object of doctors' studies. Sahi created a discourse about the way doctors dehumanized her disabled body in a laboratory like a guinea pig used for scientific experimentation. This clearly reflects Foucault's (1994) medical gaze, which looks at the body of the disabled with an objective eye, dissociating the disabled body from the knowledge of the individual. Gazing at the disabled body, dissecting it by gazing into the body, the doctor tries to explore the unexplored territory of the disabled through observation, conversation with the disabled, medical knowledge, and other medical equipment (Foucault, 1994). However, according to Foucault (1994), the patronization upon the disabled body from the doctor's perspective perpetuates the gaze, which fails to discover the natural and whole truth.

Sahi (2015a, 2015b) was aware of her sexuality and growth and conscious of the stage when a Nepali woman is ready to be married, which is when she starts her menstrual cycle. Her narratives explain how significant the monthly period of a woman is, as it opens an avenue for motherhood in a woman's life, which is almost neglected in the life of disabled women. This shows the significance of motherhood in the life of any woman and for which sex and marriage are important in Nepal. It is clear that love and sex are very desirable but, out of marriage, they have no place in the context of Nepali culture. Her narratives explore how sexually enriched a disabled body is and how fit it is for marriage. The body is filled with erotic feelings and all the desires for love and marriage. The poetic narrative reflects the idea that going through the phase of motherhood makes one forget the pain of childbirth, perhaps, even the pain of blindness.

In her narratives, Sahi (2015a, 2015b) is longing for love and marriage as she wrote, "Until the leaves sprout from it/No birds will make their nest/ No one will come to take a siesta under it" (p. 87). The narrator is comparing her disabled body, metaphorically speaking, to a naked tree that has no leaves and, therefore, no birds are coming to make a nest in her place. Sahi (2015a) discussed her body as having feelings, such as the desire for marital love and affection; however, these needs are not satisfied. She lamented about her unrequited love, a love that is never fulfilled. There are very few who understand her strong desire for love and emotions in her body. Her narratives call for all men to respect women.

In the society in which Sahi was born, a woman can easily be deemed as a whore, against which Sahi (2015b) vented her anger against men ("I love to murder you" [p. 103]) and patriarchal society which "stinks" to her everywhere (p. 103). Until society values women, it fails to recognize their ability and their feelings for love, desire, and sexuality. Sahi (2015b) spoke up against how the disabled body is viewed and requested that people stop viewing disability as a disease. Sahi also explored how people are dishonest about their view of the disabled body.

From a critical sexual theory perspective, her narratives deconstructed the idea that disabled people are devoid of love. In her narratives, Sahi (2015a, 2015b) demonstrated that love never dies but revives even more in a disabled body. Sahi's narratives bring out the absent referents to make the implicit explicit, such as her ability for love. However, people do not understand that the disabled body that is full of love, desire, and emotions. Sahi's narratives help others to understand women's disabled bodies, their desire for love and marriage, and other wishes and abilities that otherwise would have been ignored or taken for granted.

From a postcolonial theory perspective, Sahi's (2015a, 2015b) narratives decolonize the idea that the disabled do not have desires because they are asexual and pathetic. Her narratives implicitly explore the richness of reproductive organs and their growth; the narrator's monthly period; and her strong desire for love, marriage, and motherhood. Sahi (2015a, 2015b) hated how people view the disabled as if the body is in an exhibition, so she ranted against the mind-sets of people in her poetic narratives.

Furthermore, Sahi's (2015a, 2015b) discussion of how the disabled body becomes the object of the medical gaze reflects how her disabled body becomes colonized. In the wake of doctor's observation of disabled body, according to Foucault (1994), the doctor's reality of the disabled body is asserted, and the facts about the body that are dependent upon the doctor's medical gaze and his own understanding of the body of the disabled are dependent upon the doctor's sensations, perceptions, and experiences. In the relationship between the disabled body and the doctor, the former becomes colonized, and the latter becomes colonizer. In this relationship of a colonized and a colonizer, an absent referent emerges: recognizing the full potentialities of the disabled body; the thoughts, feelings, and the emotions of the disabled tend to be unrecognized and therefore invalidated.

Sahi's (2015a, 2015b) narratives speak about human cruelty: about people who, like voyeurs at a public exhibition, gaze at the disabled, talk about them as if they are inanimate objects, interfere with them, and point at them in mockery. Like a colonizer who enters the territory of the colonized and reigns, her narratives reflect on how disabled women are objectified and their private lives colonized when disabled bodies are publicly perused (Foucault, 1994; Said, 1979; Spivak, 2010).

Chapter conclusion

From critical review of their work, I discovered that the disabled women's narratives problematize the idea of disempowerment that stems from a patriarchal model depicting man as the nucleus of society and woman as a peripheral and centripetal entity. The narratives also deconstruct the idea that men are at the center and explore the independence of a woman by dismantling the hidden subalternity of a disabled woman. From a postcolonial critical theory perspective, the deconstruction of the monolithic construction of women, especially disabled women of the Third World, becomes necessary (Spivak, 1988, 2010).

Their narratives confront Foucault's (1990) biopower by challenging the social and cultural disciplinary discourse that tends to put its power over the bodies of women with disabilities. These narratives also deconstruct a social understanding of disabled women's abilities, while they explore some injustices disabled women suffer in their society. The narratives show how disabled women are marginalized in Nepal, and the absent referents are brought into view. The narratives undermine and deconstruct the idea that disabled women are asexual and unfit for marriage and sex.

Using critical sexual theory and postcolonial theory, I defined three dominant themes in assessing the narratives of disabled women: 1) the medical gaze on disabled bodies, 2) desire for love and marriage, and 3) gendered and sexist culture. These narratives explore how disabled bodies are marginalized through the gaze a disabled body receives from others, such as able-bodied people, doctors, and shamans who interpret and study the disabled body. Able-bodied people tag disabled women with asexuality. A gendered, patriarchal society dominates disabled women. These three themes can be viewed as absent referents that go unnoticed if one does not realize how disabled women have made them explicit through their narratives.

The narratives explore the medical gaze on the disabled body, even more apparent in relation to disabled women's bodies that are studied, perceived, understood, and ultimately ignored by doctors (Foucault, 1994), which is rarely questioned. Failing to question them is cloaking absent referents, such as the hidden experiences of disabled women and reinforcing the essentialist ideology of ability (Siebers, 2010). However, by reading the narratives of disabled women through the lenses of critical sexual theory and postcolonialism, one can deconstruct the ideology of ability and explore the absent referents and biopower.

In their narratives, biopower is linked to gender issues that played a crucial role in further disabling women's bodies in the culture in which all women are patronized. Critical sexual theory deals not only with gendered people but also with people of different-sexed identities, sexualities, and sexual orientations. Using critical sexual theory, one can explore how disabled narratives dismantle the idea that disabled women are asexual and without feelings. Based on a critical reading of the narratives discussed in this chapter, the essentialist categorization is inaccurate, yet necessary to deconstruct the monolithic construction of disabled women (Spivak, 1988, 2010). The narratives from disabled women pose wrenching challenges against social construction of gender and sex and invite the reader to critically look beyond the gender-sex category in which all people should fit. This deconstructs not only the monolithic perceptions of disabled women in particular but also the social construction of gender and sex in general.

Most of the narratives explore disabled women's desires for love, life, marriage, and sex, as well as their emotions. In addition, they talk about how their gender turns out to be very disadvantageous. These women's narratives have deconstructed the notion of the asexuality of disability, incapability of studying their own bodies, and patriarchal oppression. In this context, the narratives explore the relationship between society and gendered sex. The discussion of sexuality and marriage in their narratives critique the general conceptions of how the sex of disabled women is considered. These conceptions include how the family, authority, and patriarchal ideology, as well as other sociopolitical conditions such as familial organizations, economic conditions, and racial and ethnic backgrounds cloak the sexuality of the disabled. These issues have been inefficiently discussed even in the Foucauldian discourse of sexuality, which was mostly discussed in the context of the West. Thus, critical sexual theory brings the absent referents into play to further explore biopower in the context of the South East, especially Nepal.

The disabled female authors in this study have defined their sexual health and marriage. Defining their own sexual health is another way of gaining freedom from their disabled bodies. Fromm (1941) asserted that: "Sexuality offers one of the most elementary and powerful opportunities for satisfaction and happiness" (p. 99). In this context, critical sexual theory underscores the significance of sex and marriage, which have been disrupted by the existing discourses on the erotic, psychic, and social domains in Nepali society that critical theory alone would marginalize, or even ignore (King, 1992). Thus, through the narratives of these disabled women, one may explore many absent referents useful for assessing existing disability policies.

6 Assessing narratives and disability policies

In this chapter, I analyze Nepali disability policies against the narratives of select disabled Nepali female authors through the lenses of critical sexual and postcolonial theory. This chapter assesses both disability policies, including CRPD and the textual narratives of disabled women side by side, to explore if there are any mismatches that might indicate gaps in humanitarian policy. I employed Barthes' (1975) and Riessman's (2008) techniques of narrative analysis, thematic analysis, and dialogic analysis to develop findings, again with the assistance of NVivo software.

Thematic analysis

In this analysis, I discuss themes from textual narratives to understand key ideas. I also compare major themes of both disability policies and select narratives of disabled female authors of Nepal to identify similarities and differences between them. To get a feel for what could be the major themes of the disability policies, I ran a word cloud and word frequency query of all Nepali disability policies and CRPD with the help of NVivo. Both the world cloud (see Figure 6.1) and Table 6.1 present a thematic overview of existing Nepali disability policies and CRPD.

Looking at both Figure 6.1 and Table 6.1 reveals that the most frequently discussed topics are disability, people, and disabled, followed by education, social, and welfare; policy, planning, and government; and development, ministry, and children. Finally, mother and motherhood are the least frequently discussed. I generated categories such as disability and people, education and social welfare, policy and government, development and ministries, women and children, and mother and motherhood to relate what types of discussion in each Nepali disability policy fall within them. The policies are listed as follows:

- Protection and Welfare of the Disabled Persons Act 2039 (1982);
- Protection and Welfare of Disabled Persons Rules (1994);

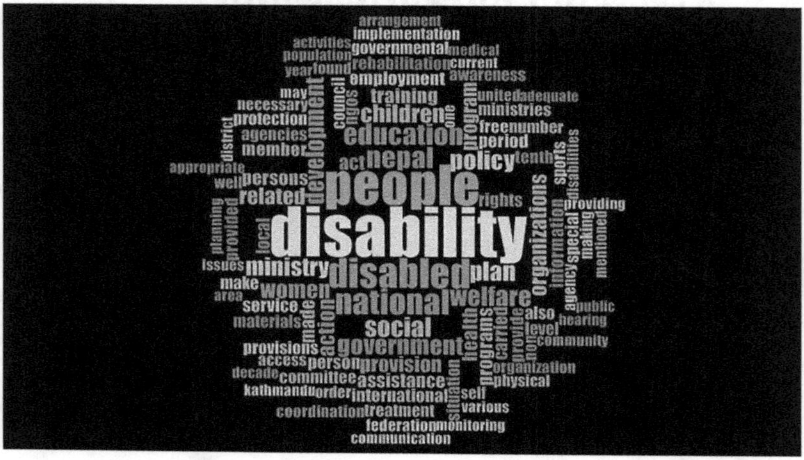

Figure 6.1 Word cloud of existing Nepali disability policies.

Table 6.1 Word frequency of Nepali disability policies

Word	Count	Weighted percentage (%)
Disability	639	3.06
People	499	2.39
Disabled	321	1.53
National	249	1.19
Nepal	196	0.94
Education	194	0.93
Social	165	0.79
Welfare	164	0.78
Policy	162	0.77
Plan	156	0.75
Government	152	0.73
Development	142	0.68
Ministry	141	0.67
Children	140	0.67
Women	131	0.63
Mother	3	0.01
Motherhood	3	0.01

Note: Weighted percentage is the frequency of the word relative to the total words counted. A word may be part of more than one group of similar words. The weighted percentage assigns a portion of the word's frequency to each group so the overall total does not exceed 100%. The total does not achieve 100% in this table because only key words specific to this study are included.

- Disabled Protection and Welfare Regulation (1996);
- Disabled Service National Policy (1996);
- Convention on the Rights of Persons with Disabilities (2006);
- National Policy and Plan of Action on Disability (2006). This policy falls under the Nepal Ministry for Women, Children, and Social Welfare; and
- Constitution of Nepal (2015).

From a thematic perspective, the policies can be categorized as follows:

- *disability and people*: All the disability policies, including the Constitution of Nepal (2015) and earlier disability regulations and welfare acts such as the Protection and Welfare of the Disabled Persons Act (1982), the Protection and Welfare of Disabled Persons Rules (1994), and the Disabled Protection and Welfare Regulation (1996) focus on people with disabilities. The policies discuss the provision of facilities for people with disabilities;
- *education and social welfare*: Disability policies discuss different facilities, education, training, and rehabilitation programs for people with disabilities;
- *policy and government*: Most of the disability policies discuss formulating policies in consultation with other agencies and organizations (Protection and Welfare of the Disabled Persons Act 2039, 1982). However, this does not reflect what kind of specific policies would be formulated;
- *development and ministries*: The policies underscore the different ministries that are responsible for providing opportunities for people with disabilities and guaranteeing their rights (see Appendix C). However, most of the rights are rights to education and access to various health services and other facilities;
- *women and children*: Some policies discuss equal representation and respect for women (National Policy and Plan of Action on Disability, 2006). However, they do not detail the way that disabled women should be respected, represented, or addressed; and
- *mother and motherhood*: The way the motherhood is discussed in the policies is more about safe motherhood at the time of delivering a baby. For example, the National Policy and Plan of Action on Disability (2006) and the CRPD (2006) discuss changing attitudes towards people with disabilities in regard to safe motherhood.

The most dominant theme of the disability policies is providing facilities for people with disabilities (see Table 6.2).

Table 6.2 Disability policies and key themes

Disabled policy by year of enactment	Relevant text*	Themes of policy narratives
Protection and Welfare of the Disabled Persons Act 2039 (1982)	The government shall, in consultation with the Social Service National Coordination Council, formulate necessary policies and programs in order to provide for the interests, treatment, and facilities concession to disabled persons under this Act, as well as provide for such other arrangements as necessary. The government may also seek the opinion of other organizations so as to formulate plans.	"Provision of facilities" "Opinion of social bodies"
Protection and Welfare of Disabled Persons Rules (1994)	15. Arrangements for education and training: 1) Any association operated at the nongovernmental or private level is to arrange education, as well as training, to disabled persons; 2) free education up to a certain level to a minimum of two descendants of a disabled person. 16. Provisions with respect to medical treatment: 1) Health of disabled persons shall be checked free of cost in hospitals; 2) There shall be arranged at least two beds free of cost in government hospitals having more than 50 beds for the treatment of disabled persons; 3) Arrangements may be made for free medical treatment of aged disabled persons above the age of 65 years and helpless disabled persons. 17. Gives priority to disabled persons at work: 1) the government shall give priority to disabled persons conducive to their education, training, and physical condition; 2) No discrimination in any form between the disabled employees and other employees is permitted. 18. Exemption from income tax. 19. Provision of disabled person service fund: 1) the government may establish a disabled person service fund for education, training, health-treatment, and rehabilitation. 20. Legal facility: In case any disabled person wishes to have legal facility of any type in the course of the hearing of a case/suit, he shall be provided with necessary legal facility through a stipendiary lawyer appointed by the government.	"Education and training" "Medical treatment" "Health treatment" "Rehabilitation"
Disabled Protection and Welfare Regulation (1996)	The Act provides different services and facilities for persons with disabilities, including educational rights, health facilities, employment opportunities, self-employment facilities, tax exemption facilities, travel facilities, and free legal aid services.	"Provision of facilities" "Employment, health, education"

Policy	Description	Themes
Disabled Service National Policy (1996)	• Provides equal opportunities in all spheres of society by empowering persons with disabilities. • Covers the following areas and services for the welfare and right of persons with disabilities: from changing attitudes toward persons with disabilities to protecting safe motherhood, to increasing awareness through the media and bringing about other rehabilitation programs.	"Empowerment" "Changing attitudes" "Safe motherhood" "Rehabilitation"
CRPD (2006)	. . . Enjoyment of the highest attainable standard of health without discrimination on the basis of disability. States Parties shall take all appropriate measures to ensure access for persons with disabilities to health services that are gender-sensitive, including health-related rehabilitation. In particular, States Parties shall: (a) Provide persons with disabilities with the same range, quality and standard of free or affordable health care and programs as provided to other persons, including in the area of sexual and reproductive health and population-based public health programs.	"Sexual and reproductive health" "Other employment and educational facilities"
National Policy and Plan of Action on Disability (2006)	16.1.1: The government, in order to protect gender discrimination against women, should protect rights of women with disabilities; the national level self-dependent organization of people with disabilities should adopt policies of full participation and equal representation in activities like management of women with disabilities, organizational training, and advocacy. 16.1.2: Special legal provisions can be made for women's benefit, protection, and welfare in relation to the right to equality. 16.1.3: In Paragraph 4(a) of Social Welfare Act 2049, the government will carry out programs to increase participation for development and to protect and promote rights and benefits of women.	"Full participation of equal representation" "Training and advocacy" "Legal provision" "Promotion of rights and benefits of women"
Constitution of Nepal (2015)	Part 3, Article 18: There would be no discrimination against people in terms of their physical condition, language, marital status, race, color, personal opinions, and disability. Article 39, Clause 9: Protect the disabled and provide facilities for people with disabilities. Article 42, Clause 3: The disabled have the rights to live a life of self-respect and the law will guarantee equal access to public facilities.	"No discrimination" "Provision of facilities" "Life of self-respect" "Equal access to public facilities"

*Verbatim from online sources of each policy and not translated by the researcher to show gender bias.

When I looked at the key themes generated from the disability policies, most of the themes are repeated in the policies that were formulated at different times. The most often repeated words are *facilities* and *provision*. The policies were developed in part by receiving opinions from social agencies that stress the need to implement medical and rehabilitation programs for the disabled. Thus, the main themes I generated from the disability policies are as follows:

- no discrimination;
- provision of facilities;
- life of self-respect;
- opinion of social bodies;
- employment, health and medication, education, training, advocacy;
- rehabilitation; and
- safe motherhood.

I also ran a word frequency query on policies from the CRPD (United Nations, 2006) of which Nepal is a signatory, including more than 100 countries. I explored the word cloud using NVivo to determine if it showed a different result than the Nepali disability policies (see Figure 6.2).

Comparing the word cloud of Figure 6.2 with Table 6.2 and the preceding list of main themes, I did not find much difference. Figure 6.1 highlights disability and people, and Figure 6.2 underscores disabilities and persons. However, Figure 6.2 seems to be more inclusive in terms of the plurality

Figure 6.2 Word cloud from CRPD analysis.

of the word disability and individual person. The CRPD (United Nations, 2006), which was ratified to address the conditions of the disabled around the world, does not include much language regarding the emotional and psychological concerns of disabled women due to differences in traditional social and culture barriers. Schaaf (2011) explained that the CRPD includes several sexually related rights. However, the sexuality rights in the convention that was adopted are far less explicit and affirmative than those included in the initial draft text (see Appendices A and D). This hints at how policies are shaped by existing social and cultural norms. In this regard, Foucault (1984) might say how abnormality and sexuality are both subject to governmentality and the government's colonizing attitudes against disabled people.

To better understand these policies, as a case study, it is important to assess the autobiographical narratives of the disabled women vis-à-vis Nepali disability policies. I assessed the themes and the concepts generated in relation to disabled women's narratives. First, I ran a word frequency and generated a word cloud from the narratives of all five disabled female authors.

In Figure 6.3, the most highlighted and repeated words are heart, love, life, society, and youth. Disability is almost dormant, and other words such

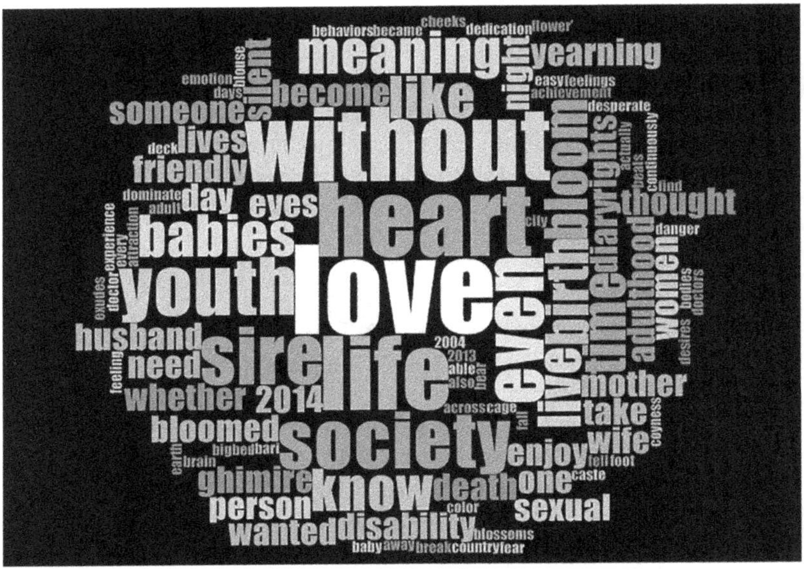

Figure 6.3 Word cloud generated from the disabled female authors' narratives.

as sexual, mother, wife, husband, babies, and yearning are dominant. If one reads the highlighted words from the top to bottom, it reads like "meaning without heart, love, life, society, know, disability." Perhaps, it can be inferred that people may view someone who has a disability as not having space for love and as not knowing what love is, or society may fail to recognize if love exists in someone with a disability. After this, I assessed the narratives of each disabled women, including key concepts evident in the narratives (see Table 6.3).

Three key themes generated from the key contents in Table 6.3 and words in Figure 6.3 are love, life, and liberty.

- *love*: This touches on sex and marriage. This theme focuses on the narratives of disabled women that touched on different aspects of disabled women's desires such as husband, being a wife or mother, getting married, sexuality, youth and other discussions related to love and affection, erotic desires, and wishes. Some of the symbols used in the narratives include "glimpses of youth and sexuality," "bloom and flower," "color of youth," "deck my forehead," and "sexual feelings";
- *life*: This theme includes the right to life and respect of life irrespective of different caste, color, creed, gender, and sex. For example, doctors or shamans experimenting on the lives of disabled people are directly or indirectly encroaching on their private life and their right to life. Some of the symbols used in the narratives include "guinea pig," "loads of mockery," "the cage of life," "life in death," and "untouchable"; and
- *liberty*: This theme underscores the social discourse on disability, reflecting disabled people's views of their disability, as well as other social beliefs and socially constructed discourses that show how these beliefs have colonized their bodies and prevented them from exercising their bodily freedom. Some of the symbols used in their narratives include "pious and free," "hysteric person," "freedom of life," and "wing sprout."

When one looks at Figures 6.1 and 6.2, Tables 6.1 and 6.2, and the list of themes, it is clear that Figures 6.1 and 6.2 highlight disability and people, while Figure 6.3 underscores heart, love, youth, society, and life of the disabled. Similarly, Table 6.1 and the list of themes emphasize organizations, ministries, governments, and other social bodies to generate opinions about the disabled bodies, while Table 6.3 emphasizes love, youth, sexuality, growth, feelings, and desires of the disabled, as well as the opinions that need to be received from the disabled bodies, not from social bodies.

Table 6.3 Select disabled narrative works and key contents

Author	Selected works	Key contents
Radhika Dahal	*Pallo Ghar ki Budhi Fupu* (*An Old Woman Next Door*) (2014a), novel *Pareliko Sandh* (*On the Edge of Eyelashes*) (2010), collection of songs *Seto Kotbhitra Kalaa Man* (*Black Hearts Inside White Jackets*) (2014b), nonfiction	Mental punishment Life in death Youth Rhododendron Heart Pool of eyes Unbuttoning the blouse of love
Jhamak Ghimire	*A Street Child's Question to her Father* (Thapa, 2009), poem *Jiwan Kada ki Phool* (*A Flower in the Midst of Thorns*) (2010), autobiography *Samaya-Bimba* (*Time-Symbols*), (2014), nonfiction	Sexual feelings Emotion Women's prestige Love and life Disability friendly Mental womb Freedom of life Wings sprout The cage of life Bloom like pear Blossoms of rhododendrons and marigolds Color of youth
Sabitri Karki	*Juneli Kabya* (*Full Moon*) (2009), collection of poems *Samarpan* (*Dedication*) (2007), collection of poems *Utpidan* (*Torture*) (2011), collection of poems	Desperate soul Untouchable Love The rights Deck my forehead
Parijat	"A Sick Lover's Letter to her Soldier" (Hutt, 2008), poem "In the Arms of Death" (Hutt, 2008), poem *Mahatahin* (*Absurdity*) (2013), novel *Shiris ko Phool* (*The Blue Mimosa*) (1980), novel "To Gopal Prasad Rimal" (Hutt, 2008), poem	Bloom, flower Hysteric person Loads of mockery Pious and free
Mina Sahi	*Atita ka Sushkeraharu* (*Whistles from the Past*) (2015a), collection of poems *Pidha Bhitra ka Chhatpati* (*A Stressful Struggle in Sorrow*) (2015b), collection of poems	Guinea pig Glimpses of youth and sexuality

Comparison of themes between policies and narratives

Comparing major themes between the fictional and nonfictional narratives of women with disabilities and disability policies, disabled women's narratives spotlight love, life, and liberty, whereas disability policies underscore rehabilitation, education and employment, health, and safe motherhood. Love for disabled women is related to marriage and sex or sexuality; life is related to gender equality irrespective of any caste, color, or ethnicity; and liberty is related to autonomy of their own bodies, emancipated from any social stigmatizations and stereotypes.

When these themes are equated with the themes generated from the disability policies, disability policies do not acknowledge social structural problems such as patriarchal gender inequality and the disabled women's capacity for sex, marriage, and sexuality. For example, rehabilitation reinforces the impression of imprisoning that might hamper women's agency for sex and marriage. Similarly, education and employment can be defined in terms of empowering facilities and services in the lives of people, but it ignores the hidden social structural problems of gender and sex inequality. The positive benefit of the policy is that there is a discussion of health and safe motherhood that looks progressive in terms of addressing some of the experiences of women with disabilities. However, to further understand, a structural analysis is needed.

Structural analysis of the narratives

The structural analysis of the narratives of the disabled is important to assessing the context of the narratives. This enables me to better understand the meaning of the statements made by the disabled women and explore the absences in which, Barthes (1975) would say, many things may happen within a sentence or between sentences. Through the structural analysis of the narratives, I explored some of the implicit meanings not stated explicitly in the narratives. I have also examined how form reflected contents and how signifiers in certain contexts explored different signifiers. I used select narratives of the disabled female authors to perform the structural analysis.

Radhika Dahal

"Society interferes with the desires and yearnings of its people and provides mental punishment throughout their lives. I need all my rights" (Dahal, 2010, p. 7). Society in the preceding narrative explores much of Nepali society, which places patriarchal ethos ahead of any decision making; the society that believes in traditional values and superstitious cultural beliefs fails to understand the experiences of disabled bodies. Rights refers to disabled people's rights to have desires and yearning that society may think immoral or impossible. Failing to perceive the rights of the disabled, society further exacerbates the conditions of the disabled. The narrator wants all those rights as they are inevitable in the lives of disabled and they are as important as they are in the lives of able-bodied people.

"Why did you make me live such a life in death?" (Dahal, 2010, p. 45). The phrase "life in death" represents suffering in life or the life a disabled woman's body has to live in. The question destabilizes the perception of the disabled body by others and establishes what the needs of the disabled body are.

"Where I bloom there opens the rhododendron of my heart" (Dahal, 2010, p. 3). Bloom signifies the opening up of youth. The rhododendron is the national flower of Nepal; the flower looks beautiful when it is in full bloom and makes the hills gorgeous. In the context where the disabled body is deemed crippled or asexual, the statement deconstructs that notion and enriches the beautiful life of the disabled filled with blooming youth.

"I wish I could swim in the pool of your eyes or I could/Enjoy in your heart unbuttoning the blouse of my love" (Dahal, 2010, p. 32). The statement is not explicit in it meaning. However, the phrase "unbuttoning the blouse of my love" signifies the erotic feelings of the narrator. The desire is there as she says, "I wish I could," but her desire perhaps would never come true as Nepali society considers sex life out of marriage to be taboo or illicit. Moreover, sex for the disabled woman is beyond societal thought in the context of Nepal.

Jhamak Ghimire

"To be without sexual feelings is to be a person without emotion" (Ghimire, 2014, p. 36). The statement deconstructs the logic that disabled people do not have sexual feelings. Sexual feelings are related to human emotions, and not to have emotions is not to be a human. This idea explicitly underscores the significance of sexual life which is hardly discussed in the lives of disabled women.

"Even if I cannot have a baby from my physical womb, I have given birth to many babies, and they all are from my brain." (Ghimire, 2014, p. 88). In a patriarchal society, if a woman cannot bear a child, she is deemed infertile and barren and is looked down upon. Even after babies are born, they are mostly recognized as being of their fathers, even in name. However, the phrase "they are all from my brain" signifies the narrator's creative works and that they are all recognized by her own name. Even if she is unable to give a physical birth to a baby, she has given birth to many poetic babies.

The text in her biography questions that even if the insects enjoy the freedom of life, why not humans? Perhaps the narrator is indicating the conditions of a disabled life that has to live in a society that does not even have the value of an insect. Sprouting wings signify youth in the body and other desires and wants that need to be fulfilled.

"Menstruation also meant the flowering of youth . . ." (Ghimire, 2010, p. 115). Menstruation has a lot of significance as it signifies the adolescent stage a female enters, carrying meaning for her youth, beauty, readiness for marriage and motherhood, and so on. However, it is called impure, and women are not allowed to touch during the menstruation cycle. In some societies, when a woman experiences her first period, she has to live far away from the house for 10 days without looking at the sunshine. There have been occasions when such separation causes death through snake bites and hyperthermia in a seclusion hut (Bhandari & Najar, 2017).

Sabitri Karki

"Mother, why did you give birth to me, I wonder whether I am meaningful to the country?" (Karki, 2007, p. 10). This question explores the position of being a daughter in Nepali society, where a son is preferred to perform rituals after the parents' demise. As the person is disabled and female, she seems to have no meaning in the society. Therefore, she wonders. Wonder not only explores the narrator's dilemma but also reminds one of the social and cultural contexts in which a woman's position is worse due to gender biases and gender inequality.

"Do not touch my hand not even by mistake now, sire! Loathed in society, untouchable is what my caste, sire!!" (Karki, 2007, p. 12). This statement is not explicit; however, an understanding of the context is useful to determining its meaning. In Nepali society, where a caste system exists, the lower castes are not treated with respect. In fact, people of lower castes are deemed untouchable or *dalit*. Thus, being disabled is deemed on par with being an untouchable. The untouchables could be the people of any lower caste who are considered to be less significant and less human in society. Satirically speaking, the narrator does not want the people of so-called higher castes to make the mistake of touching an untouchable.

"The whole world mock me today every day/Because of my yearning to deck my forehead" (Karki, 2009, p. 61). The phrase "deck my forehead," meaning to put vermillion on the forehead, has connotations related to getting married. In Nepali society, most marriages are arranged by the grooms' parents and relatives, and they are guided by the notion that it is important to have children, especially a son, to continue the lineage or to help with work (Acharya, 1987). Getting married in Karki's (2007) narratives is attached to the ideas of being someone's wife, fulfilling sexual desire, bearing children, and/or being someone's mother; these ideas are deemed to be unrealistic for disabled women. Reading between the lines of the sentences explores these aspects in the context of Nepali society.

Parijat

"My yearning for him increased, I told him without looking at him (Parijat, 1980, p. 99). The statement reflects on the closed nature of Nepali society. Even if a disabled woman experiences desire and has feelings for someone, she keeps it to herself. She cannot look a man straight in the face. However, the narrator is challenging this closed society by nevertheless expressing her desire. Although Nepali society has changed slightly, Parijat's prose represents the time during which it was written.

"I wanted to scream like a hysterical person across the night time, 'Bari, I thought I fell in love with you' but I started panicking not being able to bear the load of this mockery" (Parijat, 1980, p. 25). Women are deemed to be prone to hysterics (Foucault, 1990), and the narrator without any hesitation wants to shout with uncontrolled emotion. Like the colonized use the colonizer's language to decolonize their territory, the narrator shouts and then calls herself a hysterical person. But regardless, she expresses her love and desire, not caring who will mock her.

Using the phrase "tangible fruits of love" (translated by Hutt, 2008, p. 114), Parijat wrote about the sons that she will never have due to her disability. Her society has imposed a barrier to her getting married and having babies. It is not clear from her fictional works, as most of her first-person narrators are male, but her sexuality and sexual orientation may be coming into question as well.

Mina Sahi

"For your own experience, you made me a guinea pig" (Sahi, 2015b, p. 10). Guinea pig refers to an animal used for experimentation in a doctor's laboratory. The narrator as a disabled woman thinks of herself as a guinea pig because her body is studied, examined, tested, and interpreted.

"The day she had a period, she looked at herself in the mirror/And she thought, 'I've become an adult'" (Sahi, 2015a, p. 76). Nepali society views menstruation as impure and requires women who are menstruating to stay away from their families; however, the women themselves assign much importance and significance to menstruation. For example, the narrator sees glimpses of youth and sexuality as she experiences her menstrual cycle. She wonders why it is late for her blooming youth to invite bees.

Symbolically speaking, the narrator appears to be looking for a man to marry and mate with.

"The men are my sun and moon" (Sahi, 2015a, p. 80). This shows how men, symbolically and metaphorically speaking, in patriarchal society, are deemed guiding and enlightening figures from whom a woman succumbs to receive light, knowledge, and guidance. Even if the moon receives light from the sun, the moon also becomes a woman's guiding figure, symbolically suggesting how a woman is doubly suppressed in the patriarchal Nepali society. (Sahi, 2015a, p. 80). Critically and symbolically speaking, women seem to be devoid of love, desire, and emotions, and women's rights are not their own because they have to rely on men before making decisions about their own bodies (Sahi, 2015b).

Structural analysis of existing disability policies and the CRPD

> The Nepal Government shall in consultation with the Social Service National Coordination Council formulate necessary policies and programs in order to provide for the interests, treatment and facilities concession to the disabled persons under this Act as well to provide for such other arrangements as are deemed necessary. The Government may also seek opinion of other bodies and social associations, so as to formulate such plan.
>
> (Protection and Welfare of the Disabled Persons Act 2039, 1982, p. 3)

This policy statement highlights some of the measurable objectives of policies, such as treatment, facilities, and concessions to disabled persons, but it does not show enthusiasm for seeking out the opinions of other bodies and social associations, as shown by its use of the word *may*. The subject, government, is the actor that makes choices about whether to seek opinions from other bodies. The verb, *seek*, comes with an auxiliary verb, *may*, that shows a possibility but does not reflect the necessity to look for the opinions of other bodies and social associations, let alone the opinions of women with disabilities. Thus, the statement does not seem to address the interpretive-heterogeneous category. Similarly, the preceding statement ignores gender discrimination as it simply uses the term *disabled persons*. The policy statement has not clearly unraveled disability as it may intersect with gender and sex inequality, which means that it fails to reflect the interpretive-heterogeneous category in the typology.

"There would be no discrimination against people in terms of their physical condition, language, marital status, race, colors, personal opinions, and disability" (Constitution of Nepal, 2015, Part 3, Article 18). The disabled have the rights to live a life of self-respect and the law will guarantee equal access to public facilities (Constitution of Nepal, 2015). Barthes (1975) and Riessman (2008) emphasized the need to examine the sequence of words in statements. The preceding statements address some of the abstract concerns by indicating that there will be no discrimination against people in terms of their physical condition, marital status, and so on. However, the statements neglect a large population of women with disabilities as they fail to discuss the adoption of measures to address discrimination against women with disabilities. Similarly, the statements are unclear on how equal access will be guaranteed and how self-respect will be maintained. Self-respect is predicated on several hidden or marginalized factors, such as social and culture barriers caused by the patriarchal system and the perception of disability that is shaped and governed by social beliefs. The statements seem to reflect the interpretive-heterogeneous category by raising the issues against discrimination and mentioning the self respect of people with disabilities. However, they remain vague and unclear in terms of recognizing what self-respect entails in the gender- and caste-biased Nepali society and in understanding the conditions of women with disabilities.

"The Act will provide different services and facilities for persons with disabilities, such as educational rights, health facilities, employment opportunities, self-employment facilities, tax exemption facilities, travelling facilities, and free legal aid services" (Disabled Protection and Welfare Regulation, 1996, p. 7). This policy directly addresses the intelligible and empirical category because it enumerates services and facilities, which are measurable. However, the statement does not provide enough clues to other emotional aspects of individuals with disabilities, nor does it inform how these services discussed in the policy are affected when social structural problems are not deeply recognized.

> The government, in order to protect gender discrimination against women should protect rights of women with disability; national level self-dependent organization of people with disability should adopt policies of full participation and equal representation in activities like management of women with disability, organizational training and advocacy. 16.1.2: Special legal provisions can be made for women's benefit and protection and welfare in relation to right to equality
> (National Policy and Plan of Action on Disability, 2006, p. 83)

This is the most recent policy fully revised and amended. These statements seem to be addressing the interpretive-heterogeneous category by bringing women, gender, and disability, and especially women with disabilities, into play. However, the special discussion or the use of sex, sexuality, and gender is still not present. The policy still does not explain much about how disability intersects with gender and sex and how disability, gender, and sex are viewed in the context in which the policy is designed. The preceding policy statements recognize that gender discrimination does exist, but they do not address its underlying causes.

"Provide persons with disabilities with the same range, quality and standard of free or affordable health care and programs as provided to other persons, including in the area of sexual and reproductive health and population-based public health programs" (CRPD, 2006, Article 25). It is interesting to see that the CRPD seems to have made a great deal of progress in terms of addressing the lives of people with disabilities, and it has specifically discussed the conditions of women with disabilities. The policy uses the term *sexuality*, which has positive implications on the lives of people with disabilities. However, when one looks at the policy's underlying structure, it relates sexuality to reproductive health instead of emphasizing the sexual lives of people with different sexualities and sexual orientations. The policy does not seem to be deeply concerned with the marital lives of women with disabilities.

This policy still seems to be inadequate for Nepal, where gender inequality and caste systems are deeply rooted to worsen the sexual and marital lives of women with disabilities. It looks like disability policy makers need to rethink the gender situations within Nepalese society. In this sense, CRPD is reflective of the interpretive-heterogeneous category but still seems to be inadequate in addressing the real conditions of women with disabilities in Nepal.

Dialogic analysis

In this section, I analyze the metaphors and ideographs drawn from the narratives of the disabled women. I discuss how the choice of words in the narratives has made meaning, how critical sexual theory and postcolonial theory communicated with symbols and metaphors, and how binary oppositions were represented in the narratives. I begin by exploring some of the metaphors, symbols, and ideographs that appear in the narratives. Miller (2012) explained that: "An ideograph is a constellation of connotations capable of generating meaningful coherence, especially when tied together with story lines into a policy narrative" (p. 3). I thus examined the narratives of disabled women for ideographs and assessed those found.

While analyzing these ideographs, I discussed the personal narratives of the disabled women and the symbolic association, connotation, or meaning they communicated. The study of ideographs in the narratives is important as they are "symbolic materials that bring into view a constellation of images, emotions, values, understanding, connotations, and facts" (Miller, 2012, p. 3). The study of the ideographs as a basic unit of interpretive analysis at a symbolic level helps us understand the narratives and ascertain disability policy narratives address the emotional and psychological aspects of disabled women. I reflected on the ideographs of the disabled women's narratives and determined if policy narratives consist of, symbolically speaking, the images, emotions, values, understanding, connotations, and facts of the disabled women's narratives.

In this context, I assessed how disabled women's narratives perceive disability and related it to disability policies that define disability. When disability is defined by disability policies, the way disabled people are viewed may have both positive and negative connotations. For example, based on the narratives, disabled women have discussed how they are normally viewed: incapable of doing normal work, needing medical assistance, cursed from the past, damaged health, fallen below the human baseline, blind, lame, and deaf, devoid of feeling, lacking facilities and equal access, cannot read and write, untouchable, hysterical person, social guinea pig, subject of mockery, cage of life, mental punishment, life in death, or a desperate soul. However, using critical sexual theory and postcolonial theory shows that disabled women's narratives have deconstructed these tags to disabled people.

The personal narratives of the disabled women show who disabled people are and what they can do. Disabled women are:

- people with love, emotion, and humanity;
- people with sexual feelings and desires of motherhood;
- creative;
- pious and free;
- full of the color of youth;
- creative and can have mental wombs;
- fertile and can marry, have children, and be mothers;
- loving and can "unbutton the blouse of love".

(Dahal, 2010, p. 32)

If one looks at this imagery from the perspective of critical sexual theory and postcolonial theory, one sees how these imageries deconstruct the false belief of disability.

The ideographs that are explored in the narratives of the disabled women are hardly discussed in disability policies. The narratives of the disabled women prove that the ideology of ability is a false consciousness. Based on the disabled women's narrative, women with disabilities seem to have deconstructed the meaning of the way disability is deemed at times, such as, in their creative works, "mentally impaired" is replaced with "creative," "lack of motherhood" with "can create mental womb," "untouchable" with "pious and free," "cannot marry" with "can marry," "do not have feelings" with "can unbutton the blouse of love," "damaged health" with robust mind and with "love, emotion, and humanity," and "life in death" with "freedom within."

Through the lens of critical sexual theory, these symbols and ideographs not only signify the strength of disabled women and their fertile sexual and married life but also make one think beyond the socially constructed ideology of ability. The different imageries these women created in their narratives defy the socially constructed definitions of disability in the existing sociocultural context. The narratives of disabled women have proved that the preceding list of ideographs and their connotations are the result of social construction. Do the policy narratives recognize them?

There are some disability policies and key concepts the policies have discussed to address the condition of disabled people. The question is: Do disability policies really understand how disabled women view their disability? Do they only want medical assistance, rehabilitation, and legal provision, or do they want more than that? Or do they want these provisions or others? Do they all fit in disability policies?

Reflecting on the critical sexual theory of the disabled women's narratives in this study, most of the ideographs that the disabled female authors created have the overtones of desires for love, relationship, marriage, and sex, along with emancipation from the patriarchal culture that pervades Nepali society, and other superstitious beliefs that foster sex/gender discrimination that prevents disabled women from freely expressing their desires.

Categorical study of the narratives of the disabled women

Based on the narratives of the disabled women, I have created five themed categories within which their ideas can be summarized. These categories are the colonized bodies of the disabled; negligence and ignorance of the disabled; gender/sex of the disabled; sexuality, marriage, love, and beauty of the disabled; and emancipation and rights of the disabled.

Colonized bodies of the disabled

Most of the narratives of the disabled female authors discuss how their bodies are colonized. Ghimire (2010) was not happy with the system in Nepal and how women are treated, and she wondered what the situation of disabled women could be like. This lack of self-agency shows how a disabled woman's body is colonized.

Similarly, Sahi (2015a) wrote about how the state treats the disabled person like a guinea pig in a doctor's laboratory. Symbolically speaking, a guinea pig is an animal that is used for experimentation. The guinea pig's body is colonized and observed, studied, analyzed, and interpreted, and the animal often dies prematurely. The lines here explain more clearly how the body is colonized. "For your own experiment, you made me a guinea pig/ Shame on your ignorant knowledge . . ./In your laboratory, my future is lost . . ." (Sahi, 2015a, p. 86).

Similarly, Nepali social beliefs have colonized disabled bodies as explored through the narratives of the disabled women. Nepali culture is based on the Hindu religion and other social beliefs, including superstitions. *Saudamini* (Disability, 2011), a collection of articles by disabled people and others, published some of the statements made about women that are often over-heard, directly or indirectly, that indicate how marginalized women are:

- "If a woman is lazy, she might give birth to a daughter" ;
- "Shit, she gave birth to a daughter!";
- "A son is a lamp of the house; a daughter is a bitch whose death would make no difference";
- "A daughter should not be lazy"; and
- "A daughter-in-law should not sleep until late."

(p. 27)

Disabled women are deemed untouchables, and they are loathed in society as they are not viewed as complete humans. In her poem "Samarpan" (Dedication), Karki (2007) wrote how social beliefs and Nepali culture have inculcated negative attitudes against disabled people. The perception of the disabled is limited, thus affecting the body of the disabled.

Ghimire (2010) wrote about how people indoctrinate superstitious cultural beliefs and social bias into children's minds, and then these children are often incapable of overcoming social prejudices. These beliefs colonize the conditions of the disabled. Nepal needs policies for women with disabilities that remove these false social beliefs. The narratives analyzed in this study challenge the socially constructed understanding of disability, and they also challenge policy makers for failing to incorporate these ideas into disability policies to effectively address the conditions of disabled women.

Negligence and ignorance of the disabled

The narratives in this study highlight how family and society are negligent about the conditions of disabled women. Society does not realize that disabled women have become doubly disabled due to this negligence. How disabled women are neglected can be understood through their narratives. Dahal (2010, 2014a, 2014b) wrote that society interferes with the desires and yearnings of the people and inflicts mental punishment throughout their lives. Society encroaches on the lives of the disabled, and this encroachment becomes disturbing to disabled people in ways that society, and even their families, fail to understand.

This negligent behavior of the family is extremely damaging. In this context, Ghimire wrote in her poetic narrative: "Why did you damage me/on a corner of the street?" (Thapa, 2009, p. 126). In this poem, Ghimire blamed her father for not being able to provide the environment that the disabled body was seeking. This, according to Ghimire, is the negligence of the family, and the government does not seem to be deeply concerned about this neglect.

Similarly, Karki (2011) wrote the following poetic lines: "Why is the priceless life so heavy on my shoulders? Nobody hears my vow, who should I talk to, sir?" (p. 38). This narrative reflects the bitter truth and grieving reality of women with disabilities. Life is priceless, but it feels heavy on the shoulders of women with disabilities and nobody wants to hear the disabled women's voice, which thus falls on deaf ears.

Ignorance of ability in disabled people echoes in the narratives of the five disabled Nepali female authors. It shows that disabled women are more than able and capable of doing much by themselves, sometimes even more so than the able-bodied. In her poem, "Disability," collected in *Utpidan*, Karki (2011) wrote about why the skills and abilities of the disabled are refused and neglected. The narratives of the disabled women reflect on the failure of disability policies that do not address the negligence of society regarding women's disabled bodies.

Gender/sex of the disabled

Ghimire (2014) discussed some textual interpretations of women in Hindu moral books. According to Ghimire (2014), these religious books write about the natural traits that women are guilty of having – "to tell lies," "not to have courage," "to be greedy and stupid," being "impious," and having "ignorance" (p. 74). Similarly, Ghimire wrote about the discriminatory norm that a husband is encouraged to marry another woman if his wife becomes disabled, also suggested by the National Code of Law (2016). However, there is no such policy for women who have the same fate.

Nepali society is patriarchal, and a husband is to be pleased by his wife. Religion has cemented this idea of a wife being loyal to her husband. This patriarchal ethos of Nepali society has worsened the condition of women with disabilities, and this is demonstrated in the narratives. For example, in the novel *Seto Kotbhitra Kalaa Man* (*Black Hearts Inside White Jackets*) (2010), Dalal wrote: "If you wanted to kill me, why didn't you slit my throat? Why did you make me live such a life in death?" (pp. 44–45).

These expressions speak up against a patriarchal society that dominates women. Ghimire (2014) called many men rapists as she wrote: "Rapists are all the time vying to rape innocent women whether that is for sexual satisfaction or to dominate women's prestige" (p. 76). This statement strongly expresses an anguish and frustration against a patriarchal society that is gendered and sexist.

Ghimire (2010) wrote about kinship and sexual discrimination by addressing her grandmother. Her grandmother thought that it was wrong to give birth to a daughter because she thought without a son she had no journey to heaven after her death. This clearly shows the patriarchal nature of Nepali society.

Ghimire (2010) also wrote how her father treated her badly. She explained that if she did not obey her father's orders, he would scold her saying, *alchhine sanpe*, meaning unfortunate bad creature, and he would begin cursing her. He thought she was dumb and that only he was clever and had a right to laughter and happiness. Ghimire wrote that she suffered from a gendered society. As long as the patriarchal society remains unchanged, Ghimire realized that disabled women will suffer.

Sexuality, marriage, love, and beauty of the disabled

Sexuality, marriage, beauty, and love are dominant themes in most of the narratives of the disabled female authors in this study. Their narratives emphasize these themes as absent referents, or tools to liberate, emancipate, and unfetter themselves from the bondage of society. It shows how disabled women are aware of their bodies and sexuality that society ignores and that the disability policy also fails to incorporate. In "Ashaktata" (Inability), Karki (2009) wrote about her yearning to "deck my forehead" when the "adulthood set its foot in my heart" (p. 61).

It is clear that society makes fun of disabled women's sexuality and doubts their desire to be mothers. Some of the questions the poetic narratives ask include: Don't the disabled have feelings? Don't they have desires for love? These are critical questions that challenge socially constructed notions about disabled women that they cannot have sex and do not have the capacity to bear a child.

The poetic narratives provide a sense of how normal disabled people are. Dahal (2010) wrote: "Where I bloom there opens the rhododendron of my heart, Where I go or visit there continuously beats my heart" (p. 3). She expressed her love in these lines: "I wish I could swim in the pool of your eyes or I could, Enjoy in your heart unbuttoning the blouse of my love" (Dahal, 2010, p. 32). Here are beautiful images and metaphors she used, such as "unbuttoning the blouse of love". She looked kindly toward love and sexual activity. This idea deconstructs the notion that only abled people are sexually active.

Ghimire (2014) wrote: "Actually, all humans have the matter of sex, and no one can be separated from it. It is because I also have youth and adulthood. To be without sexual feelings is to be a person without emotion" (p. 36). In her autobiography, Ghimire (2010) explored her happiness for having her fully developed bodily parts – breasts, buttocks, and vagina – which made her life colorful. Ghimire said that she was like pear and guava plants in full bloom, like the blossoms of rhododendrons and marigolds. Her cheeks bloomed with the color of youth. Ghimire's view of beauty is not only based on physical beauty but also on inner beauty.

Love, yearning, and desire are recurring themes in most of the disabled women's narratives. Although Parijat is a woman, most of her protagonists are first-person narrators, and the first-person narrator is a man. One may wonder about the gender identity or sexuality of Parijat. It was difficult for Parijat to question her sexual orientation, and it was not easy for her to be open about her sexual orientation. In most of her fictional narratives, the first-person narrator is a male who has a strong desire for love with a woman. One of the female narrators in the novel says to the first-person narrator, "My yearning for him increased, I told him without looking at him 'then do not let that bloom without any purpose, there must be some meaning to be a flower'" (Parijat, 1980, p. 99). Sahi (2015a) also expressed the same inner feelings of her love and sexuality in the poem, "Memory of my Birth House" (p. 76).

These narratives explore how happy the women become when they looked at themselves in the mirror and saw themselves as sexy and beautiful, when they found the adolescence in themselves and their well-developed bodily parts. Looking at it critically, the disabled women want society to understand how important love, sexuality, marriage, and beauty are in women's lives, and that their disability should not be an issue preventing them from celebrating a life of love, partnership, and romance. Existing disability policies do not discuss the significance of sex, marriage, and sexuality in the lives of the disabled besides a minor word on the reproductive rights of women.

Emancipation and rights of the disabled

Another dominant theme of the disabled women's narratives in this study is individual freedom or emancipation. Most of their narratives fight the injustice and bondage of the disabled woman. Karki's (2007) poem entitled "Anonymous Martyr" questions what it means to be a woman and questions her ability to have a meaningful existence in a patriarchal society (p. 10).

Karki's desire to live longer and meaningfully shows her right to the expression of freedom and freedom of life. Parijat expressed her freedom and emancipation from the bondage of her own body, as well as the bondage that people in her society and the imprisonment that her father created. Parijat wanted to be free even though her own physical body was incapable of moving freely (Prasai, 2010).

Ghimire (2010) expressed similar views on personal freedom in her poetic expression about freedom and being out of the "cage"; that is, she wanted to be emancipated from the place where she was chained (Ghimire, 2010, p. 244)

Dialogic analysis of disability policies

The Protection and Welfare of the Disabled Persons Act (1982) used terms such as "disabled person" and "helpless disabled person" (p. 1).

> Disabled person means a Nepalese citizen who is physically or mentally unable or handicapped to do normal daily life-works. This expression also includes a blind, one-eyed, deaf dumb, dull, crippled, limb, lame, handicapped with one leg broken, handicapped with one hand broken, or a feeble-minded person.
>
> (Protection and Welfare of the Disabled Persons Act, 1982, Article 1.a.)

The definition represents disabled people as crippled, lame, handicapped, or feebleminded. A *cripple* is someone who is unable to move or walk properly, and the word fits as an adverb for a disease such as "a crippling disease." Metaphorically and symbolically speaking, these words imply that to be disabled is to suffer from a disease. Similarly, *feebleminded* is used to describe someone who is unable to think or act intelligently. These words tend to reinforce the social stigmas faced by people with disabilities.

These words set certain social norms for disabled people. Thus, such word choices, instead of acknowledging the disabling sociocultural structure under which disabled people must operate, tend to reinforce social biases and structural problems between the so-called abled and the disabled. These policies consciously or unconsciously encourage disability not as a difference but as a disease. After some amendments, the Protection and Welfare of Disabled Persons Rules (1994) was enacted. This law created a few more services for people with disabilities, but it did not significantly improve the definition of disability.

The National Policy and Plan of Action on Disability (2006) was enacted as the most recent disability policy in action, and the policy also contained some ideas that are found within the CRPD. However, the policy did not clearly define the concept of disability. The policy addressed the health and empowerment of the disabled, including a specific topic on women and disability that discusses health and safe motherhood, but it did not clarify how disability is defined or viewed. In other words, the policy has succeeded in creating new strategies to address the needs of people with disabilities but failed to communicate what disability really is in the Nepali sociocultural context. Not being able to define what disability means in Nepal may cause the government to fail to protect and promote the rights of persons with disabilities.

After assessing the narratives of women with disabilities, exploring different themes in existing Nepali disability policies, and examining the CRPD of which Nepal is a signatory, it is evident that there is some mismatch between the way disability is defined in policies and the way women with disabilities have defined their own disabled bodies and fertility. Disability policies do not seem to have discussed the important issues that address the psychological and emotional concerns of the disabled. Even the CRPD discusses sexuality much lesser than what was proposed before it was ratified and published (see Appendix D).

Disability policies seem to include some specific policies aimed at addressing the conditions of the disabled. However, the themes generated from existing disability policies do not include the emotional dimensions of women, and these issues need to be addressed. Disability policies seem to be the result of multiple conflicting policy agendas.

7 Testing the typology of narratives

Based on the analysis of the narratives of women with disabilities and disability policies, I revisited the typology of narratives proposed in Table 1.1 to discover policy gaps or mismatches. The findings did not alter the proposed typology. Table 1.1 explained how disability policies rarely reflect the gendered lives of women with disabilities. The findings are further discussed through the lens of critical sexual theory that links to the discussion of Foucault's (1990) biopower and other discursive practices in the context of Nepal.

Intelligible and empirical category

I did not find enough data in the narratives by women with disabilities that discuss the lack of different services in education, employment, and other services that the disability policies have guaranteed, and there were few mentions of the lack of implementation and government effectiveness. Very few of the narratives discussed the lack of health services and the lack of disability-friendly infrastructures and institutions such as schools and hospitals. The authors did not discuss the difficulties arising out of the lack of disability-friendly services or facilities, nor did they discuss extensively advocating or underscoring their rights for education, employment, and health and legal services. However, in the context of Nepal, there are several geographical challenges and difficulties, and there is not enough disability-friendly infrastructure nor is there easy access to health, education, and employment services (Lamichhane, 2012a, 2014). Policies seem to be highly geared toward addressing the concerns that are explicitly visible.

Empirical and observational category

I found that most of the disability policies discussed education, employment, and health for people with disabilities. The policies seem to be more concerned with the geographical challenges of the country and the need for people with disabilities to access different services. The policies address apparent and visible problems that can be measured and observed rather than the individual or unseen problems that are abstract and deemed taboo (e.g., sex and marriage for women with disabilities).

The analyzed policies also did not specifically discuss women with disabilities besides some health and reproductive policies (Ministry of Health and Population, 2011). However, looking into the report of the Ministry of Health (2017), I did not find any gender or sex issues of women with disabilities being addressed. The Demographic and Health Survey (Ministry of Health, 2017) implied that Nepali society still believes sex is a taboo. When it comes to the sex lives of women with disabilities, they are highly gendered, and policies lag behind and do not explain gender issues outside the normative standards of the society. This further reinforces gendered stereotypes and what Foucault (1990) called disciplinary discourses that guide institutions and institutional practices. The discourses define the institution of marriage, sex, and love and partnership for women with disabilities.

Interpretative and heterogeneous category

In this category, I found a lot of experiences about how the issues of gender and sex influenced the disabled women's lives and how they are misunderstood and stereotyped. Their narratives helped me better understand how disability intersects with gender and other social characteristics that tend to further dehumanize women with disabilities. I also learned that women with disabilities deconstructed and challenged the stereotypes of themselves as asexual.

Regarding Foucault's (1990) biopower, most of the narratives in this category reflect the emancipation of the authors from sociocultural stereotypes that tend to view women with disabilities as asexual and unfit for marriage. They exercised their power by bringing their marginalized voices of love, partnerships, affections, sex, and marriage into their writing, thus resisting societal biopower.

Discussing the beauty of their bodies and dismantling the cultural perception of the disabled body, the women with disabilities dispel the myth of asexuality in this category. Their narratives reversed the discourse that Foucault (1984) called "polymorphous techniques of power" (p. 60) that "produce" effects of truth (p. 298). These five women with disabilities in Nepal have, through their narratives, broken the silence and taboos, dismantling the paradigm of viewing Nepali women with disabilities, and even breaking the citadel of the disciplinary discourse, the social rules that limit human behavior and reality in Nepal (Foucault, 1984).

Interpretative and reflexive category

I investigated narratives in this category to identify any gender policies that addressed the concerns of women with disabilities or acknowledged disability that intersects with gender and other social characteristics such as race, ethnicity, caste, and culture. After a thorough analysis of the narratives of women with disabilities and disability policies, I was unable to find any effective gender policies that addressed the narratives. I concluded that there are some policy mismatches that fail to address different gender and marital issues of women with disabilities in Nepal. The policies do not seem to acknowledge that women with disabilities have deconstructed the myth of disability as asexual and unfit for marriage. I did not find any policies that clearly defined gender and sex in the context of Nepal.

Discussion of the typology

From the proposed typology, it can be extrapolated that disability is a social construction intertwined with regulation and Foucault's (1990) concept of normalization. Foucault described that people are not only externally disciplined into acting in certain ways but also self-disciplining. These disciplinary practices directly and indirectly silence the voice of the marginalized, hence silencing the sex lives of women with disabilities in this context, as sexuality is discussed in negative normative terms within familial and institutional settings.

Foucault (1990) argued that we are constituted within discourses, making one unable to think outside the box; thus, women with disabilities in this context tend to be labeled as asexual and rely on this to feel protected. This discourse shapes perceptions and social rules that silence the marginalized. Foucault (1984) wrote: "Silence itself – the things one declines to say or is forbidden to name . . . is less the absolute limit of discourse . . . than . . . an integral part of the strategies that underlie and permeate discourses" (p. 300). Thus, not acknowledging disabled sexuality is a way of regulating it.

Most organizations that work for people with disabilities consider gender equality in terms of education, employment, and health services, and there are hardly any organizations that discuss the issues of love, relationships, and partnerships for women with disabilities. The situation of those with disabilities is bleak and reflects that the attitude toward the disabled, especially women with disabilities, is negative. Further, when it comes to the issues of love and partnership in the lives of women with disabilities, these are deemed taboo, and society remains unwilling to entertain these subjects.

Sex as a taboo is reflected in disability policies as well. The CRPD (United Nations, 2006) was formulated while taking into account the fact that there were no strong and legally binding international laws for the disabled, and that government programs, policies, and budgets did not prioritize the needs of the disabled. The CRPD aims to recognize people with disabilities as full and equal members of society, with obligatory provisions to protect and promote the rights of these people on an equal basis with others. The CRPD considers different emotional aspects of people with disabilities that deal with their marriage and sexuality, yet it does not reflect the issues of women with disabilities in the third category of the typology, let alone in other disability policies within the local context of Nepal. Even in the CRPD, the terms *sex* and *sexuality* are used more in relation to reproductive health than to the biological needs of disabled people, and the words are not used frequently (Schaaf, 2011). Ruiz (2017) examined how the CRPD has sustained a protective, medical, and gender binary model to address the sexual and reproductive rights of persons with disabilities. Ruiz recommended moving away from a narrow approach to sexuality, understanding that sex/gender is more fluid and shifting, recognizing the ability of persons with disabilities to express and act upon desire consensually, and bringing into the discussion issues of sexual orientation and gender identity.

Until one looks into the historical or sociopolitical powers that define disability, it is further naturalized through existing dominant discourses, such as that the disabled are asexual or incapable and that they need medical or other interventions to fix their problems. Foucault (1969) wrote that discourses are created by social and economic arrangements and conditions that can be transformed. By diagnosing those discourses that perpetuate societal problems, Foucault (1969) suggested that one can explore biopower, the historical effects and sociopolitical operations of power on the body. All disability policies regulate the perceptions of disability while not acknowledging the gendered lives of women with disabilities in Nepal. The typology suggests that policies are unable to acknowledge women with disabilities outside how they are socially labeled. Foucault (1969) and Butler (2006) argued that people are constituted within discourses and unable to think outside of how they are labeled. For example, there are hardly any policies that discuss sex as a biological need for women with disabilities in the policy contexts of Nepal, reflecting how society labels disabled women as asexual.

Some reproductive policies (Ministry of Health and Population, 2011) discuss sexual rights focusing on family life, with no mention of sexuality and sexual agency. such policies fail to acknowledge that women with disabilities are sexual beings with equal rights to sexual pleasure, intimacy, love, friendship, relationship, and sexual and reproductive choices. Thus, I found that these polices reinforce how disabled women tend to be deemed asexual, therefore excluding them from a life of active sexuality and denying them the opportunity of motherhood.

The discourse of viewing women with disabilities as asexual (Foucault, 1990) includes policies that are made to address their sexual and reproductive rights. Therefore, these policies are hegemonic (Ingram, Schneider, & deLeon, 2007). Such policies exert disciplinary power over their bodies, as Foucault (1990) metaphorically suggested, preventing them from using their biological rights and limiting them to what Stivers (2002) called private spaces. From the postcolonial perspective, disciplinary power is another way of "othering" them. Similarly, the policies viewed through the lens of critical sexual theory and Foucault's (1990) biopower explain how the state, supported by scientific discourse, "brought life and its mechanisms into the realm of explicit calculations and made knowledge-power an agent of the transformation of human life" (Foucault, 1984, p. 17), thus speaking of women with disabilities of Nepal in this context.

In summary, most of the disability policies in the context of Nepal fall in the second category of the typology – empirical and observational – and most of the narratives of women with disabilities fall in the third category of the typology – interpretative and heterogeneous. This means the policies in the second category only address the disability issues discussed in the first category – intelligible and empirical – and the issues discussed in the third category tend to be left unaddressed. This suggests policy mismatches reflecting the power of discursive practices that create "truth" on the conditions of women with disabilities in this context. Policies seem to have ignored how disability intersects with gender or sex and other social characteristics that further stereotype disabled women in Nepal. However, the analysis of the disabled women's narratives in this study shows that these women have deconstructed the stereotypes, thus interrupting the power discourse and changing the gendered and sexist perception of their lives.

The results can inform other disability policies in other sociocultural contexts. They can also be discussed in the South Asian contexts that share many sociocultural practices and perceptions that people have of women with disabilities.

8   Conclusions

In this book, the study examined the autobiographical and fictional narratives of Nepali disabled female authors Radhika Dahal, Jhamak Ghimire, Sabitri Karki, Parijat, and Mina Sahi to assess disability policies in Nepal and determine whether they reflect the needs of disabled women. The study analyzed the narratives of these authors and explored the absent referents, that is, what a woman's disabled body learned and gained from Nepali society that sees the disabled body as asexual and unfit for marriage and motherhood. I assessed the narratives in comparison to existing disability policies, including the CRPD (United Nations, 2006) and other health and reproductive polices. The disabilities of the women authors varied: Radhika Dahal has a spinal injury, Jhamak Ghimire is born with cerebral palsy, Sabitri Karki and Mina Sahi are blind, and Parijat was physically incapacitated.

Most of the narratives explored motherhood, beauty, and sexuality, in addition to sociocultural beliefs and the patriarchal ethos that further disabled them, oppressed their rights, and colonized their bodies and freedom. Motherhood, beauty, and sexuality are viewed as central attributes for women in Nepali society, where marriages are arranged and where having a beautiful wife capable of bearing children is the goal of all men. However, most of the narratives explored how society denied these essential roles of being a female and expressing one's true sexuality.

The narratives invited us to understand motherhood, love, and sex in the life of women with disabilities and also to explore the role of gender and sex in the context of Nepal that shapes people's understanding of ability. The narratives of women with disabilities in Nepal show how they experience a double disadvantage because they are viewed as being part of the inferior sex. Biased cultural beliefs, what Foucault (1990) referred to as disciplinary discourses and biopower, prevented them from exploring their desires for love and marriage. Clearly, there is an absence of attention to the sexual and emotional aspects of disabled women in Hindu society or disabled women in the South Asian context in general. The narratives also show how disabled women are the victims of people's sympathy, and how their bodies and their sexual lives are colonized by how they are perceived.

Marginalized, disabled women can be understood as a subaltern group, or as colonized ones who have "no history and cannot speak, the subaltern as female is even more deeply in shadow" (Spivak, 2010, p. 83). Spivak (2010) proposed multiple understandings (signifiers) of *satee* (a practice among some Hindu communities where a recently widowed woman, either voluntarily or by force, immolates herself on her deceased husband's pyre). Spivak explained that *satee* is defined by either Hindu leaders or British colonizers but never from the *satee*-performing women themselves; metaphorically speaking, the voice of the women with disabilities, as compared to *satee*, should be heard to understand women with disabilities and other emotional and psychological aspects of them. "Between patriarchy and imperialism, subject-constitution and object formation, the figure of the woman disappears, not into a pristine nothingness, but into a violent shuttling which is the displaced figuration of the third world woman caught between tradition and modernization" (Spivak, 2010, p. 102). In this context, based on the narratives of disabled women, it is apparent that the body of the disabled is colonized and that important themes of their lives such as love, sex, and marriage have become absent referents that need to be explored from a critical sexual theory perspective.

Understanding the disabled women expressed in the words they used to write about their bodies, sexuality, and lived experiences, deconstructs the notion that disabled women are asexual and without feelings. The narratives help one understand marriage and sexuality, illness, pain, and disability in the lives of these disabled women and can reshape these women's views of their bodies. The narratives show how society, culture, and the body are linked in the disabled woman and how they deconstruct the ideology of ability that stigmatizes disabled people. Stigmatization excludes people who do not fit the category of normal. Such people fall in the lower rank of a social hierarchy, where the subaltern group falls. They are minorities, others, physically and mentally different, or in the case of Nepal, untouchables, lower caste, sinful, and asexual. The narratives have problematized these categories for the disabled and advocate for the ability of the disabled saying that the disabled are sexual, ready for marriage, and capable of doing anything an able-bodied person can do. The problematization has provided plenty of room to explore disability policies that need to acknowledge disabled women's voices. The research shows that besides the discussion of rehabilitation, education, and employment, there are many other emotional and psychological aspects of being a disabled woman to consider in disability policies.

The symbols and ideographs extracted from the disabled female authors' narratives not only reflect their conditions but also explore their emotional and psychological dimensions, including their desire for love, sex, and marriage, and how sex and gender play a crucial role in defining the nature of disability. Their narratives have deconstructed the social perceptions of disabled women. While matching themes generated out of the narrative of women with disabilities in comparison with Nepali disability policies, it is evident that the government fails to address gender stereotypes that interfere with the emotional and psychosocial needs of disabled women. There are many potentialities of women with disabilities that the policies rarely recognize. The idea that a woman can be a mother, symbolically speaking, by giving birth to poetry is an innovative approach that can be brought into the discussion of the disabled women's perception of their disabled bodies.

Bishwakarma (2013, 2014) underscored the ineffectiveness of Nepali disability policies. Some of the policies created to address the conditions of the disabled are not well executed because the disabled are deprived of their rights. However, the rights of the disabled are guaranteed in disability policies. Gender discrimination also plays a role in marginalizing disabled women (Bishwakarma, 2014). Bishwakarma (2014), who is a *dalit* woman, proposed that how the disabled are viewed or treated is worse than the paucity of disabled-friendly infrastructure. Bishwakarma (2014) argued that disability laws and policies, such as the Nepali legislation of 1982 and 2006, as well as others, are more sympathetic than viable for the disabled, and do not bring about any positive change in viewing the disabled.

Devkota, Murray, Kett, and Groce (2018) wrote about nonaccessible beds during delivery, insensitive providers with negative attitudes, and abusive behavior: ". . . inadequate knowledge and experience in providing services to the people with disabilities as well as unwelcoming health facility environment made services particularly inaccessible to women with disabilities" (p. 2). Although these are enforcement issues, perhaps agencies that serve people with disabilities should have a written gender policy. Such policies might honor the sexual, marital, and reproductive health of women with disabilities. Moreover, in the context of Nepal specifically or South Asia in general, the policies are mostly written for all people with disabilities, not specifically for women with disabilities. It remains significant that the policies need to focus on different needs for women with disabilities and must address existing social taboos and stereotypes.

Defining disability as a disease can sentence an individual to internal exile when they cannot move or walk out of the house. This reflects the colonial relationship between the able and the disabled. This relationship results in mental pathologies and negative attitudes toward the disabled that can produce ambivalence on the part of disabled people. As among colonized people who have ambivalence regarding who they really are, disabled people also experience identity ambivalence.

The prevalence of gendered sexist attitudes is another colonial factor affecting the bodies of disabled women. The law of karma renders disabled women impure and unfortunate, and when they go through menstruation, they are considered even more impure. Thus, policies need to address these lapses beyond acts of benevolence, such as showing kindness to and sympathizing with people with disabilities, instead of merely addressing employment and physical infrastructure while failing to acknowledge gender and cultural roles that dehumanize women with disabilities and their needs.

The narratives of disabled women show that Nepal is incapable of acknowledging the disabled in relation to sexuality and marriage because of socially constructed mind-sets. In Carew, Braathen, Swartz, Hunt, and Rohleder's (2017) study on the sexual lives of low- and middle-income people with disabilities in the context of low- and middle-income countries, many nondisabled women had positive attitudes toward sexuality and believed that disabled women could marry and have children. Tanabe, Nagujjah, Rimal, Bukania, and Krause (2015), in the context of Nepal, Kenya, and Uganda, underscored the intersection of sexual and reproductive health and disability in humanitarian settings. They reported that there were barriers, especially for women with disabilities, to have access to sexual and reproductive health rights and their rights in relationships. In an American context, Samowitz (2010) emphasized the need for policies that support the sexuality and sexual needs of people with disabilities. They proposed that organizations working with disabled people should have specific gender policies, or as Samowitz (2010) preferred, sexual policies. Regarding sexuality, Foucault (1990) discussed how the discourse on sexuality is formulated and how its power prevails over policy. Foucault's (1990) biopower helps one understand how and why sexuality in the CRPD (United Nations, 2006) might have been compromised and not mentioned anywhere in CRPD policies, and also in existing disability policies in Nepal. When sexuality is viewed in relation to women, it is silenced as disabled women are deemed more vulnerable, sexually passive or asexual, and dependent. This study explored the relationship of gender and disability and found that gendered stereotypes limit disabled women's life choices and insults their sexuality.

Women with disabilities are afraid, feel shame, and have insecurities about their sexuality (Bernert & Ogletree, 2013). The barrier lies not in the inability to develop responsible social and sexual behaviors but in the misapprehensions and collective negative attitudes of some administrators, professionals, family members, and the uninformed general public who continue to support outdated laws and public and agency policies that deny the basic rights of people with disabilities. Reflecting on the narratives of women with disabilities in relation to existing disability policies, this study provides insights into the complex relationships between the traditional role of gender and sex and women with disabilities. Assessing the narratives of disabled women and reflecting on existing disability policies, I found that the policies are not effective enough to address the gendered society, therefore worsening the conditions of disabled women.

Understanding gender and sexuality is important in bringing the rights of women with disabilities into a discourse concerning their sexuality. In the context of Nepal, there are some national health policies that aim to address people's right to sexuality, which are mostly for reproductive health and health services (Ministry of Health and Population, 2011). Nonetheless, sexual and reproductive health problems continue to affect the lives of women in Nepal (Ministry of Health, 2017).

As discussed, in the context of Nepal, women's access to resources and opportunities are shaped by gender bias and social stereotypes. Their sexuality is controlled in the name of chastity and family honor that tend to further marginalize minorities. Sex as a taboo in Nepal causes a reluctance to discuss and address sexual health issues. People are stigmatized if they do not conform to social normative standards. Women are economically dependent on men, and there are unequal power relations based on gender and other traditional practices and beliefs. This invites a discussion on the sociocultural analysis of power structures. Gender and sexuality need to be understood in the context of power and social relationships. Sexuality should be acknowledged as a desire of the body. Policies should incorporate sexuality within the discourse of power that currently controls individual sexuality. This will help one understand sexuality by moving beyond the issues of reproduction and understanding sexual rights for social and sexual freedom. In this way, policies can address gender issues while addressing the rights of women with disabilities, thus making them more inclusive.

Finally, the Nepali disabled female authors in this study help expose the lack of disability policies that address the gendered sex issues of disabled women and the issues of love, life, and liberty, as well as reflect the conditions of women with disabilities in other nations. These authors are able to subvert the negative images of disabilities and replace them with images that claim their beauty, difference, humanity, and sexuality in a way that is public. This realization may help policy makers, sexuality activists, agencies working for people with disabilities, and academic scholars to be aware of disability as it intersects not only with gender and sex but also in other societal contexts.

Appendices

Appendix A

Convention on the Rights of Persons with Disabilities select policies

Article	Policy Summary
Article 6: Women with Disabilities	1. States Parties recognize that women and girls with disabilities are subject to multiple discrimination, and in this regard shall take measures to ensure the full and equal enjoyment by them of all human rights and fundamental freedoms. 2. States Parties shall take all appropriate measures to ensure the full development, advancement and empowerment of women, for the purpose of guaranteeing them the exercise and enjoyment of the human rights and fundamental freedoms set out in the present Convention.
Article 12: Equal Recognition Before the Law	1. States Parties reaffirm that persons with disabilities have the right to recognition everywhere as persons before the law. 2. States Parties shall recognize that persons with disabilities enjoy legal capacity on an equal basis with others in all aspects of life. 3. States Parties shall take appropriate measures to provide access by persons with disabilities to the support they may require in exercising their legal capacity. 4. States Parties shall ensure that all measures that relate to the exercise of legal capacity provide for appropriate and effective safeguards to prevent abuse in accordance with international human rights law. Such safeguards shall ensure that measures relating to the exercise of legal capacity respect the rights, will and preferences of the person, are free of conflict of interest and undue influence, are proportional and tailored to the person's circumstances, apply for the shortest time possible and are subject to regular review by a competent, independent and impartial authority or judicial body.

(Continued)

(Continued)

Article	Policy Summary
	The safeguards shall be proportional to the degree to which such measures affect the person's rights and interests. 5. Subject to the provisions of this article, States Parties shall take all appropriate and effective measures to ensure the equal right of persons with disabilities to own or inherit property, to control their own financial affairs and to have equal access to bank loans, mortgages and other forms of financial credit, and shall ensure that persons with disabilities are not arbitrarily deprived of their property.
Article 25 Health	Health States Parties recognize that persons with disabilities have the right to the enjoyment of the highest attainable standard of health without discrimination on the basis of disability. States Parties shall take all appropriate measures to ensure access for persons with disabilities to health services that are gender-sensitive, including health-related rehabilitation. In particular, States Parties shall: (a) Provide persons with disabilities with the same range, quality and standard of free or affordable health care and programs as provided to other persons, including in the area of sexual and reproductive health and population-based public health programs.

Source: United Nations (2006).

Appendix B
Relevant Nepali ministries

- *Ministry for Women, Children, and Social Welfare.* The National Coordination Committee was formed under the leadership of the Minister for Women, Children, and Social Welfare to amend the Disabled Persons Protection and Welfare Act (1982). The government initiated a situation analysis regarding disability status and extended especial education to cover many districts in urban and rural areas. The government declared inclusive education as policy effective 2004 and started implementing it in over "210 schools of 22 districts, 340 primary recourse class in 73 districts" (National Policy and Plan of Action on Disability, 2006, p. 51). The government created a scheme to provide loans for disabled people. The disabled were to be allocated 5% of the total financial resources of local governments, and a further 5% was to be taken from government employment programs to pay for such loans. Since the early 1980s, many NGOs and government programs accepted and implemented community-based rehabilitation (CBR) programs for people with disabilities throughout Nepal. In 1999, the Ministry of Women, Children, and Social Welfare and the CBR National Network jointly developed a national strategy to enhance and implement CBR programs in Nepal (Crishna & Prajapati, 2008).
- *The Ministry of Education.* The Ministry of Education was charged with bestowing integrated education opportunities for children with disabilities. However, most of them were concentrated in the larger municipalities (Crishna & Prajapati, 2008).

Appendix C

CRPD first draft versus ratified draft

Domain	Draft Presented by Committee Chair at Fifth Session	Convention as Adopted
Marriage and family life	That persons with disabilities are not denied the equal opportunity to [experience their sexuality,] (3) have sexual and other intimate relationships [through a legal marriage] and experience parenthood [in accordance with the national laws, customs and traditions in each country].	(a) The right of all persons with disabilities who are of marriageable age to marry and to found a family on the basis of free and full consent of the intending spouses is recognized; The rights of persons with disabilities to decide freely and responsibly on the number and spacing of their children and to have access to age-appropriate information, reproductive and family planning education are recognized, and the means necessary to enable them to exercise these rights are provided.
Awareness-raising	States parties shall take [all] appropriate and effective measures to promote awareness, and provide education and information to the public in accessible formats, aimed at changing negative perceptions and social prejudices towards [sexuality marriage and parenthood] [in all matters of marriage and family relations] for persons with disabilities.	States Parties undertake to adopt immediate, effective and appropriate measures: (a) To raise awareness throughout society, including at the family level, regarding persons with disabilities, and to foster respect for the rights and dignity of persons with disabilities; (b) To combat stereotypes, prejudices and harmful practices relating to persons with disabilities, including those based on sex and age, in all areas of life.

| Freedom from exploitation, violence, and abuse | States parties shall take all appropriate legislative, administrative, social, educational and other measures to protect persons with disabilities both within and outside the home, from [all forms of exploitation, violence and abuse] [all forms of harm, including] [all forms of exploitation, violence and abuse, including abandonment, violence, injury or mental or physical abuse, abduction, harassment, neglect or negligent treatment, maltreatment or exploitation, including economic and sexual exploitation and abuse]. | 1. States Parties shall take all appropriate legislative, administrative, social, educational and other measures to protect persons with disabilities, both within and outside the home, from all forms of exploitation, violence and abuse, including their gender-based aspects.

States Parties shall also take all appropriate measures to prevent all forms of exploitation, violence and abuse by ensuring, inter alia, appropriate forms of gender- and age-sensitive assistance and support for persons with disabilities and their families and caregivers, including through the provision of information and education on how to avoid, recognize and report instances of exploitation, violence and abuse. States Parties shall ensure that protection services are age-, gender- and disability-sensitive. |
| Right to health | Provide persons with disabilities with the same range and standard of [affordable/free] health [and rehabilitation services] as provided other persons, [including sexual and reproductive health services] and population-based public health programs (4). | Provide persons with disabilities with the same range, quality and standard of free or affordable health care and programs as provided to other persons, including in the area of sexual and reproductive health and population-based public health programs. |

Source: United Nations (2006).

References

Abel, C. F., & Sementelli, A. J. (2005). Evolutionary critical theory, metaphor, and organizational change. *Journal of Management Development, 24*(5), 443–458. https://doi.org/10.1108/02621710510598454

Acharya, M. (1987). Changing division of labor and participation. In J. W. Bjorkman (Ed.), *Changing division of labor* (pp. 128–140). New Delhi, India: Manohar.

Acharya, M. (1994a). *Gender and democracy in Nepal*. Kathmandu, Nepal: Tribhuvan University.

Acharya, M. (1994b). Political participation of women in Nepal. In N. Chowdhury & B. Nelson (Eds.), *Women and politics worldwide* (pp. 479–495). New Haven, CT: Yale University Press.

Acharya, M. (1994c). *The statistical profile on Nepalese women: An update in the policy context*. Kathmandu, Nepal: Institute for Integrated Development Studies.

Acharya, M., & Bennett, L. (1979). *The status of women in Nepal* (Vols. 1–5). Kathmandu, Nepal: Center for Economic Development and Administration and Tribhuvan University.

Acharya, S. (2017). Disability law implementation: The role of NGOs and INGOs in Nepal. *National Judicial Academy Law Journal, Nepal, 11*, 1–25. http://dx.doi.org/10.2139/ssrn.2831810

Acharya, T. (2017). Nepal Himalaya: Women, politics, and administration. *Journal of International Women's Studies, 18*(4), 197–208. Retrieved from https://vc.bridgew.edu/jiws/vol18/iss4/14

Acharya, T. P. (2005, July 7). Gender discrimination and women empowerment. *The Rising Nepal*, p. 6.

Adams, C. J. (2015). *The sexual politics of meat: A feminist-vegetarian critical theory*. New York, NY: Bloomsbury Publishing.

Addlakha, R. (2007). How young people with disabilities conceptualize the body, sex and marriage in urban India: Four case studies. *Sexuality and Disability, 25*(3), 111–123. https://doi.org/10.1007/s11195-007-9045-9

Adorno, T. W. (1991). *The culture industry: Selected essays on mass culture*. London, UK: Routledge.

Agger, B. (1993). *Gender, culture, and power: Toward a feminist postmodern critical theory*. Westport, CT: Praeger Publishers.

Allen, A. (2013). *The politics of our selves: Power, autonomy, and gender in contemporary critical theory*. New York, NY: Columbia University Press.

Ashworth, K. (2001). *Caught between the dog and fireplug*. New York, NY: Georgetown University Press.

Bamberg, M. (2003). Stories, tellings, and identities. In C. Daiute & C. Lightfoot (Eds.), *Narrative analysis: Studying the development of individuals in society* (pp. 135–157). London, UK: Sage.

Bamberg, M. (2011). Who am I? Narration and its contribution for self and identity. *Theory and Psychology, 21*(1), 1–22. https://doi.org/10.1177/0959354309355852

Bamberg, M., & Georgakopoulou, A. (2008). Small stories as a new perspective in narrative and identity analysis. *Text and Talk, 28*(3), 377–396. https://doi.org/10.1515/TEXT.2008.018

Barthes, R. (1975). An introduction to the structural analysis of narrative. *New Literary History, 6*(2), 237–272. Retrieved from www.jstor.org/stable/468419

Beasley, C. (2005). *Gender and sexuality: Critical theories, critical thinkers*. Thousand Oaks, CA: Sage.

Bennett, L. (1983). *Dangerous wives and sacred sisters: Social and symbolic roles of high caste women in Nepal*. New York, NY: Columbia University Press.

Berger, P., & Luckmann, T. (1966). *The social construction of reality*. London, UK: Penguin.

Berkowitz, E. D. (1979). *Disability policies and government programs*. New York, NY: Praeger Publishers.

Berkowitz, M., Johnson, W. G., & Murphy, E. H. (1976). *Public policy toward disability*. New York, NY: Praeger Publishers.

Bernert, D. J. (2011). Sexuality and disability in the lives of women with intellectual disabilities. *Sex and Disability, 29*(2), 129–141. https://doi.org/10.1007/s11195-010-9190-4

Bernert, D. J., & Ogletree, R. J. (2013). Women with intellectual disabilities talk about their perception of sex. *Journal of Intellectual Disability Research, 57*(3), 240–249. https://doi.org/10.1111/j.1365-2788.2011.01529.x

Bhambani, M. (2003). Societal responses to women with disabilities in India. In A. Hans & A. Patri (Eds.), *Women, disability and identity* (pp. 282–295). New Delhi, India: Sage.

Bhandari, P. (2013, August 14). *A case study: Nepal mental health policy and law*. Retrieved from http://mentalhealthworldwide.com/2013/08/nepal-mental-health-policy-and-law-nepal/

Bhandari, R., & Najar, N. (2017, July 9). Shunned during her period, Nepali woman dies of snakebite. *The New York Times*. Retrieved from www.nytimes.com/

Birkenholtz, J. V. (2018). *Reciting the Goddess: Narratives of place and the making of Hinduism in Nepal*. New York, NY: Oxford University Press.

Bishwakarma, S. (2013, September 8). Apangata and adhikar, disability and rights. *Kantipur Daily*, p. 6.

Bishwakarma, S. (2014, July). Apangata and bartaman awastha, disability and present situation. *Kantipur Daily*, Kathmandu, Nepal.

Bochner, A. P., & Ellis, C. (1995). Telling and living: Narrative co-construction and the practices of interpersonal relationships. In W. Leeds-Hurwitz (Ed.), *Social approaches to communication* (pp. 201–213). New York, NY: Guildford.

Boje, D. M. (1991). The storytelling organization: A study of story performance in an office supply firm. *Administrative Science Quarterly, 36*(1), 106–126. Retrieved from www.jstor.org/stable/2393432

Box, R. C. (2005). *Critical social theory.* Armonk, NY: M. E. Sharpe.

Boylan, E. (1991). *Women and disability.* London, UK: Zed Books.

Brinkley, A. (2010). *The unfinished nation: A concise history of the American people.* New York, NY: McGraw-Hill Education.

Brodd, J. (2003). *World religions: A voyage to discovery.* Winona, MN: Saint Mary's Press.

Brouwers, C., Brakel, W. H. V., Cornielje, H., Pokhrel, P., Dhakal, K. P., & Banstola, N. (2012). Quality of life, perceived stigma, activity and participation of people with leprosy-related disabilities on south-east Nepal. *Disability, CBR and Inclusive Development, 22*(1), 16–34. doi:10.5463/DCID.v22i1.15

Bruner, J. (1991). The narrative construction of reality. *Critical Inquiry, 18*(1), 1–21. Retrieved from www.jstor.org/stable/1343711

Burkhauser, R. V., & Daly, M. C. (2002). Policy watch: Disability policy in a changing environment. *The Journal of Economic Perspectives, 16*(1), 213–224.

Burr, V. (2003). *Social constructionism.* New York, NY: Routledge.

Butler. J. (2006). *Gender trouble.* New York, NY: Routledge.

Cameron, M. M. (1998). *On the edge of the auspicious: Gender and castes in Nepal.* New York, NY: University of Illinois Press.

Carbado, D., & Gulati, M. (2003). The law and economics of critical race theory. *The Yale Law Journal, 112*(7), 1757–1828.

Carew, M., Braathen, S. H., Swartz, L., Hunt, X., & Rohleder, P. (2017). The sexual lives of people with disabilities within low- and middle-income countries: A scoping study of studies published in English. *Glob Health Action, 10*(1). doi:10.108 0/16549716.2017.1337342

Chase, S. E. (2005). Narrative inquiry: Multiple lenses, approaches and voices. In N. K. Denzin & Y. S. Lincoln (Eds.), *The Sage handbook of qualitative research* (3rd ed., pp. 651–679). Thousand Oaks, CA: Sage.

Christ, C. P. (2006). Why women need the Goddess: Phenomenological, psychological, and political reference. In E. Hackett & S. Haslanger (Eds.), *Theorizing feminism* (pp. 257–266). New York, NY: Oxford University Press.

Collins, P. H. (1998). *Black feminist thought: Knowledge, consciousness, and the politics of empowerment* (2nd ed.). New York, NY: Routledge.

Constitution of Nepal, 2015. *Ministry of Law, Justice and Parliamentary Affairs of Nepal.* Kathmandu, Nepal.

Cooper, H. (2010). *Research synthesis and meta-analysis: A step-by-step approach* (4th ed.). Thousand Oaks, CA: Sage.

Corbin, J., & Strauss, A. (2008). *Basics of qualitative research: Techniques and procedures for developing grounded theory* (3rd ed.). Thousand Oaks, CA: Sage.

Cranny-Francis, A., Waring, W., Stavropoulos, P., & Kirkby, J. (2003). *Gender studies: Terms and debates.* New York, NY: Palgrave Macmillan.

Creswell, J. W. (2007). *Research design: Qualitative, quantitative, and mixed methods approaches* (2nd ed.). Thousand Oaks, CA: Sage.

Crishna, B., & Prajapati, S. B. (2008). Comparative policy brief: Status of intellectual disabilities in Nepal. *Journal of Policy and Practice in Intellectual Disabilities*, *5*(2), 133–136. https://doi.org/10.1111/j.1741-1130.2008.00161.x

Cuthbert, K. (2017). You have to be normal to be abnormal: An empirically grounded exploration of the intersection of asexuality and disability. *Sociology*, *51*(2), 241–257. https://doi.org/10.1177/0038038515587639

Czarniawska, B. (2004). *Narratives in social science research*. London, UK: Sage.

Dahal, R. (2010). *Pareliko sandh (On the edge of eyelashes)*. Kathmandu, Nepal: Manjushree Printing Press.

Dahal, R. (2014a). *Pallo ghar ki budhi fupu (An old woman next door)*. Kathmandu, Nepal: SNS Press.

Dahal, R. (2014b). *Seto kotbhitra kalaa man (Black hearts inside white jackets)*. Kathmandu, Nepal: Shamisam Prakashan Griha.

Dalmiya, V. (2000). Loving paradoxes: A feminist reclamation of the goddess Kali. *Hypatia*, *15*(1), 125–150. Retrieved from www.jstor.org/stable/3810514

DeJong, G., & Lifchez, R. (1983). Physical disability and public policy. *Scientific American*, *248*(6), 26–37. http://dx.doi.org/10.1038/scientificamerican0683-40

Denhardt, R. (1999). *Public administration: An action orientation*. Fort Worth, TX: Harcourt Brace.

Devkota, H. R., Murray, E., Kett, M., & Groce, N. (2018). Are maternal health care services accessible to vulnerable group? A study among women with disabilities in rural Nepal. *PLoS One*, *13*(7), 1–20. https://doi.org/10.1371/journal.pone.0200370

Dhungana, B. M. (2006). The lives of disabled women in Nepal: Vulnerability without support. *Disability and Society*, *21*(2), 133–146. https://doi.org/10.1080/09687590500498051

Dirar, U. C. (2007). Colonialism and the construction of national identities: The case of Eritrea. *The Journal of Eastern African Studies*, *1*(2), 256–276. https://doi.org/10.1080/17531050701452556

Disability. (2011). *Saudamini, a Journal*, *2*(7), 12–15. Kathmandu, Nepal.

Disabled Protection and Welfare Regulation, Nepal, 1996. *Ministry of Women and Children*. Kathmandu, Nepal.

Doe, T. M. (1997). Gender issues in disability policy. *Journal of Disability Policy Studies*, *8*(2), 239–247.

Election to the Members of the Constituent Assembly Act, Nepal, 2007. Kathmandu, Nepal. Retrieved from http://aceproject.org/ero-en/regions/asia/NP/nepal-election-of-the-members-of-constituent

Emmett, T., & Alant, E. (2006). Women and disability: Exploring the interface of multiple disadvantage. *Development Southern Africa*, *23*(4), 445–460. https://doi.org/10.1080/03768350600927144

Ensler, E. (2001). *The vagina monologues* (Acting ed.) [Script]. New York, NY: Dramatist Play Service, Inc.

Epstein, D., O'Flynn, S., & Telford, D. (2001). "Othering" education: Sexualities, silences, and schooling. *Review of Research in Education*, *25*, 127–179. Retrieved from www.jstor.org/stable/1167323

Ewick, P., & Silbey, S. S. (1998). *The common place of law: Stories from everyday life*. Chicago, IL: University of Chicago Press.

Feldman, M. S., Sköldberg, K., Brown, R. N., & Horner, D. (2004). Making sense of stories: A rhetorical approach to narrative analysis. *Journal of Public Administration Research and Theory, 14*(2), 147–170. doi:10.1093/jopart/muh010

Forester, J. (1980). Critical theory and planning practice. *Journal of the American Planning Association, 46*(3), 275–286. https://doi.org/10.1080/01944368008977043

Forester, J. (1993). *Critical theory, public policy and planning practice.* Albany, NY: SUNY Press.

Forum of Women and Law Development, Nepal, 2006. Kathmandu, Nepal. Retrieved from https://fwld.org/publications/?cat=14

Foucault, M. (1969). *The archaeology of knowledge.* London, UK: Routledge.

Foucault, M. (1975). *Discipline and punishment: The birth of the prison.* New York, NY: Random House.

Foucault, M. (1984). *The Foucault reader.* New York, NY: Pantheon Books.

Foucault, M. (1990). *The history of sexuality: An introduction* (Vol. 1) (R. Hurley, Trans.). New York, NY: Random House.

Foucault, M. (1994). *The birth of clinic.* New York, NY: Random House.

Fraser, N. (1985). What's critical about critical theory? The case of Habermas and gender. *New German Critique, 35,* 97–131. Retrieved from www.jstor.org/stable/488202

Freud, S., & Strachey, J. (Eds.). (1989). *Civilization and its discontents.* New York, NY: W. W. Norton and Company.

Fromm, E. (1941). *Escape from freedom.* New York, NY: Farrar and Rinehart.

Garland-Thomson, R. (1997). *Extraordinary bodies.* New York, NY: Columbia University Press.

Gautam, S. (2017). The event of sexual pleasure as de-subjectivization in Foucault and Kamasutra. *South Asian Review, 34*(3), 19–34. https://doi.org/10.1080/0275 9527.2013.11932938

Gerschick, T. J. (2000). Toward a theory of disability and gender. *Journal of Women in Culture and Society, 25*(4), 1262–1268. Retrieved from www.jstor.org/stable/3175525

Ghai, A. (2002). Disabled women: An excluded agenda of Indian feminism. *Hypatia, 17*(3), 49–66. Retrieved from www.jstor.org/stable/3810795

Ghai, A. (2003). *(Dis)embodied form: Issues of disabled women.* New Delhi, India: Har-Anand Publications.

Ghimire, J. (2010). *Jiwan kada ki phool (A flower in the midst of thorns)* (N. Sharma & S. Sharma, Trans., G. R. Bhattarai, Ed.). Kathmandu, Nepal: Oriental Publication House.

Ghimire, J. (2014). *Samaya-bimba (Time-symbols).* Kathmandu, Nepal: Sabdahar Creations.

Giami, A. (1987). Coping with the sexuality of the disabled: A comparison of the physically disabled and mentally retarded. *International Journal of Rehabilitation Research, 10*(1), 41–48. http://dx.doi.org/10.1097/00004356-198703000-00004

Gilbert, H., & Tompkins, J. (1996). *Post-colonial drama: Theory, practice, politics.* London, UK: Routledge.

Goffman, E. (1963). *Stigma: Notes on the management of spoiled identity.* New York, NY: Simon and Schuster.

Goodley, D. (2013). Dis/entangling critical disability studies. *Disability and Society*, *28*(5), 631–644. https://doi.org/10.1080/09687599.2012.717884

Gray, A. (2003). *Research practice for cultural studies: Ethnographic methods and lived cultures*. London, UK: Sage.

Greene, S. (2015). Gender and sexuality in Nepal: The experience of sexual and gender minorities in a rapidly changing social climate. *Independent Study Project Collection*, (2093). Retrieved from http://digitalcollections.sit.edu/cgi/viewcontent.cgi?article=3115&context=isp_collection

Griffiths, M., & Macleod, G. (2008). Personal narratives and policy: Never the twain? *Journal of Philosophy and Education*, *42*(1), 121–142. https://doi.org/10.1111/j.1467-9752.2008.00632.x

Groce, N. E. (1997). Women with disabilities in the developing world: Arenas for policy revision and programmatic change. *Journal of Disability Studies*, *8*(1/2), 177–193. https://doi.org/10.1177/104420739700800209

Groce, N. E., London, J., & Stein, M. A. (2014). Inheritance, poverty, and disability. *Disability and Society*, *29*(10), 1554–1568. https://doi.org/10.1080/09687599.2014.969831

Grossman, B. R. (2003, September). *Understanding disability and sexual identity development: Theory, method, and future directions*. Paper presented at the First Disability Studies Association Conference, Lancaster University, Lancaster, UK.

Gubrium, J. F., & Holstein, J. A. (2009). *Analyzing narrative reality*. Thousand Oaks, CA: Sage.

Habermas, J. (1987). *The theory of communicative action* (3rd ed.). Boston, MA: Beacon Press.

Habermas, J. (1990). *Moral consciousness and communicative action*. Cambridge, MA: MIT Press.

Habermas, J., & Seidman, S. (1989). *Jurgen Habermas on society and politics: A reader*. Boston, MA: Beacon Press.

Hafiz, Y. (2017, December 6). The fascinating world of Kumari, Nepal's Living Goddesses. *The Huffington Post*. Retrieved from www.huffingtonpost.com/

Hahn, H. (1985). Disability policy and the problem of discrimination. *American Behavioral Scientist*, *28*(3), 293–318. https://doi.org/10.1177/000276485028003002

Hans, A., & Patri, A. (Eds.). (2003). *Women, disability, and identity*. New Delhi, India: Sage.

Haveman, R. H., Halberstadt, V., & Burkhauser, R. V. (1984). *Public policy toward disabled workers: Cross-national analysis of economic impacts*. Ithaca, NY: Cornell University Press.

Herz, M., & Johansson, T. (2012). "Doing" social work: Critical consideration on theory and practice in social work. *Advances in Social Work*, *13*(3), 527–540.

Heyes, C. (2015). When does social learning become cultural learning? *Journal of Neuropsychology*, *20*(22), 1–14. https://doi.org/10.1111/desc.12350

Hiranandani, V. (2005). Towards a critical theory of disability in social work. *Journal of Critical Social Work*, *6*(1). Retrieved from www1.uwindsor.ca/criticalsocialwork/towards-a-critical-theory-of-disability-in-social-work

Hood, C. (1989). Public administration and public policy: Intellectual challenges for the 1990s. *Australian Journal of Public Administration*, *48*(4), 346–358. https://doi.org/10.1111/j.1467-8500.1989.tb02235.x

Horkheimer, M. (1976). Traditional and critical theory. In P. Connerton (Ed.), *Critical sociology: Selected readings* (pp. 206–224). Harmondsworth, UK: Penguin.

Huberman, A. M., & Saldaña, J. (2014). *Qualitative data analysis: A methods sourcebook.* Thousand Oaks, CA: Sage.

Hutt, M. (2008). *Himalaya voices: An introduction to modern Nepali literature.* Berkeley, CA: University of California Press.

Ingram, H., Schneider, A., & deLeon, P. (2007). Social construction and policy design. In P. A. Sabatier (Ed.), *Theories of the policy process* (pp. 93–126). Boulder, CO: Westview Press.

Ingstad, B. (1999). The myth of disability in developing nations. *The Lancet, 354*(9180), 757–758. https://doi.org/10.1016/S0140-6736(99)06049-3

Ingstad, B., & Reynolds-Whyte, S. (2007). *Disability in local and global worlds.* Berkeley, CA: University of California Press.

Institute of Applied Phenomenology. (2010). *Applied phenomenology.* Retrieved from www.appliedphenom.org/applied-phenomenology.html

Jackson, P. (1998). Theorizing gender and sexuality. In S. Jackson & J. Jones (Eds.), *Contemporary feminist theories* (pp. 120–134). New York, NY: New York University Press.

Jarmul, D. (2006, March 26). Women at war in Nepal. *Duke Today.* Retrieved from http://today.duke.edu/2006/03/nepal.html

Jefferson, G. (1978). Sequential aspects of storytelling in conversation. In J. Schenkein (Ed.), *Studies in the organization of conversational interaction* (pp. 219–248). New York, NY: Academic Press.

Judson, O. (2009, November 3). License to wonder [Opinion]. *The New York Times.* Retrieved from http://opinionator.blogs.nytimes.com/2009/11/03/license-to-wonder/

Karki, S. (2007). *Samarpan (Dedication): A collection of poems.* Kathmandu, Nepal: Jaleswari Shrestha.

Karki, S. (2009). *Juneli kabya (Full moon).* Kathmandu, Nepal: A.B. Secretarial and Prints PVT.

Karki, S. (2011). *Utpidan (Torture).* Kathmandu, Nepal: Bagalamukhi Offset Press.

Kelly, T. (2004). Unlocking the iron cage: Public administration in the deliberative democratic theory of Jurgen Habermas. *Administration and Society, 36*(1), 38–61. https://doi.org/10.1177/0095399703257268

Kim, E. (2011). Asexuality in disability narratives. *Sexualities, 14*(4), 479–493. https://doi.org/10.1177/1363460711406463

King, C. R. (1992). To have or not to have sex in critical theory: Sexuality in the early writings of Wilhelm Reich and Erich Fromm. *Mid-American Review of Sociology, 16*(2), 81–91. Retrieved from www.jstor.org/stable/23254548

Lamichhane, K. (2012a). Disability and barriers to education: Evidence from Nepal. *Scandinavian Journal of Disability Research, 15*(4), 311–324. https://doi.org/10.1080/15017419.2012.703969

Lamichhane, K. (2012b). Employment situation and life changes for people with disabilities: Evidence from Nepal. *Disability and Society, 27*(4), 471–485. https://doi.org/10.1080/09687599.2012.659462

Lamichhane, K. (2014). Social inclusion of people with disabilities: A case from Nepal's decade-long civil war. *Scandinavian Journal of Disability Research, 17*(4), 287–299. https://doi.org/10.1080/15017419.2013.861866

Lamichhane, K., Paudel, D. B., & Kartika, D. (2014). *Analysis of poverty between people with and without disabilities in Nepal*. Tokyo, Japan: JICA Research Institute.

Langellier, K. M. (1989). Personal narratives: Perspectives on theory and research. *Text and Performance Quarterly*, *9*(4), 243–276. https://doi.org/10.1080/104629 38909365938

Langellier, K. M. (1999). Personal narrative, performance, performativity: Two or three things that I know for sure. *Text and Performance Quarterly*, *19*(2), 125–144. https://doi.org/10.1080/10462939909366255

Levi-Strauss, C. (1995). *Myth and meaning: Cracking the code of culture*. New York, NY: Schocken.

Liasidou, A. (2014). Intersectional understandings of disability and implications for a social justice reform agenda in education policy and practice. *Disability and Society*, *28*(3), 299–312. https://doi.org/10.1080/09687599.2012.710012

Limbu, S. T., & Jha, K. (2018, August 10). Gender, nation, and women's honour. *The Kathmandu Post*. Retrieved from http://kathmandupost.ekantipur.com/

Lipsky, M. (2010). *Street-level bureaucracy: Dilemmas of the individual in public services* (30th anniversary expanded ed.). New York, NY: Russell Sage.

Loomba, A. (2001). *Colonialism/postcolonialism*. London, UK: Routledge.

Lyotard, J. F. (1984). *The postmodern condition: A report on knowledge* (G. Bennington & B. Massumi, Trans.). Minneapolis, MN: University of Minnesota Press.

Mackinnon, C. (2006). Desire and power. In E. Hackett & S. Haslinger (Eds.), *Theorizing feminism* (pp. 262–273). New York, NY: Oxford University Press.

Mahoney, M. R. (1991). Legal images of battered women: Redefining the issues of separation. *Michigan Law Review*, *90*(1), 1–94. Retrieved from https://repository. law.miami.edu/cgi/viewcontent.cgi?article=1388&context=fac_articles

Mailloux, S. (1995). Interpretation. In F. Lentricchia & T. McLaughlin (Eds.), *Critical terms for literary study* (pp. 121–132). Chicago, IL: University of Chicago Press.

Malhotra, R., & Rowe, M. (2013). *Exploring disability identity and disability rights through narratives: Finding a voice of their own*. London, UK: Routledge.

Mandelbaum, J. (1989). Interpersonal activities in conversational storytelling. *Western Journal of Speech Communication*, *53*(2), 114–126. https://doi.org/10.1080/ 10570318909374295

Mandelbaum, J. (1993). Assigning responsibility in conversational storytelling: The interactional construction of reality. *Text*, *13*(2), 247–266. https://doi.org/10.1515/ text.1.1993.13.2.247

Marx, K., & Engels, F. (1848). *The communist manifesto*. London, UK: Workers' Educational Association.

McAdams, D. (1993). *The stories we live by: Personal myths and the making of the self*. New York, NY: Guildford.

McCabe, M. P. (1999). Sexual knowledge, experience and feelings among people with disability. *Sexuality and Disability*, *17*(2), 157–170. https://doi.org/10.1023/ A:1021476418440

McCabe, M. P., Cummins, R. A., & Deeks, A. A. (2000). Sexuality and quality of life among people with physical disability. *Sexuality and Disability*, *18*(2), 115–123. https://doi.org/10.1023/A:1005562813603

McRuer, R., & Mollow, A. (2012). *Sex and disability*. New York, NY: Duke University Press.

McSwain, C. J. (2002). A public service life. *Journal of Public Affairs Education*, *8*, 5–8.

Meekosha, H., & Shuttleworth, R. P. (2009). What's so critical about critical disability studies? *Australian Journal of Human Rights*, *15*(1), 47–75. https://doi.org/10.1080/1323238X.2009.11910861

Memmi, A. (1991). *The colonizer and the colonized*. Boston, MA: Beacon Press.

Miller, H. (2012). *Governing narratives*. Tuscaloosa, AL: The University of Alabama Press.

Ministry of Health. (2017, November). *Nepal: Demographic and health survey 2016*. Kathmandu, Nepal: Author. Retrieved from www.dhsprogram.com/pubs/pdf/fr336/fr336.pdf

Ministry of Health and Population, Nepal, 2011. Kathmandu, Nepal. retrieved from https://www.mohp.gov.np/eng/

Mishler, E. G. (1995). Models of narrative analysis: A typology. *Journal of Narrative and Life History*, *5*(2), 87–123. http://dx.doi.org/10.1075/jnlh.5.2.01mod

Mishler, E. G. (2005). Patients' stories, narratives of resistance, and the ethics of humane care: A la recherche du temps perdu. *Health*, *9*(4), 231–251. https://doi.org/10.1177/1363459305056412

Mostov, J., & Ivekovic, R. (2006). *From gender to nation*. New Delhi, India: Zubaan Books.

National Code of Law, Nepal, 2016. *Nepal Law Commission*. Kathmandu, Nepal.

National Policy and Plan of Action on Disability. (2006). *Nepal ministry for women, children, and social welfare*. Kathmandu, Nepal.

Nelson, B. J., & Chowdhury, N. (1994). *Women and politics worldwide*. New Haven, CT: Yale University Press.

Nepal, A. (2018). *Swasthani brata katha*. Kathmandu, Nepal: Ananda.

New Era for National Planning Commission. (2001). *A situation analysis of disability in Nepal: Executive summary of Disability Sample Survey 2001*. Retrieved from https://rcrdnepa.files.wordpress.com/2008/05/a-situation-analysis-of-disability-in-nepal-2001.pdf

Nhanenge, J. (2011). *Ecofeminism: Towards integrating the concerns of women, poor people, and nature into development*. Lanham, MD: University Press of America.

Nosek, M. A., Howland, C. A., Young, M. E., Georgiou, D., Rintala, D. H., Foley, C. C., . . . Smith, Q. (1994). Wellness models and sexuality among women with physical disabilities. *Journal of Applied Rehabilitation Counseling*, *25*(1), 50–58.

Olivelle, P. (2005). *Manu's code of law*. New York, NY: Oxford University Press.

Oliver, M. (1986). Social policy and disability: Some theoretical issues. *Disability Handicap and Society*, *1*(1), 5–17. https://doi.org/10.1080/02674648666780021

Oliver, M. (1996). *Understanding disability: From theory to practice*. London, UK: Palgrave Macmillan.

O'Toole, C. J., & Bregante, J. L. (1992). Disabled women: The myth of asexual women. In S. S. Klein (Ed.), *Sex, equity, and sexuality in education* (pp. 273–304). Albany, NY: SUNY Press.

Parijat. (1980). *Shiris ko phool (The blue mimosa)*. Kathmandu, Nepal: Sajha Prakashan.

Parijat. (2013). *Mahatahin (Absurdity)*. Kathmandu, Nepal: Sajha Prakashan.

Percy, S. L. (1993). Challenges and dilemmas in implementing disability rights policies. *Journal of Disability Policy Studies*, *4*(1), 41–63. https://doi.org/10.1177/104420739300400103

Prasad, P. (2005). *Crafting qualitative research: Working in the post positivist traditions*. New York, NY: M. E. Sharpe.

Prasai, N. R. (2010). *The legend of literature: A biography of Parijaat*. Kathmandu, Nepal: Ekta Publications.

Protection and Welfare of the Disabled Persons Act 2039, Nepal, 1982. Ministry of Women and Children. Kathmandu, Nepal.

Protection and Welfare of Disabled Persons Rules. (1994). Ministry of Women and Children. Kathmandu, Nepal.

Raghavan, P., & Vora, A. (Eds.). (2016, June). *A critical examination of sexuality discourses in India*. New Delhi, India: Nirantar. Retrieved from www.nirantar.net/uploads/files/A%20Critical%20Examination%20of%20Sexuality%20Discourses%20in%20India%20pdf.pdf

Rahman, A., & Ahmed, P. (1993). Women with disabilities in Bangladesh. *Canadian Woman Studies*, *13*(4), 47–48. Retrieved from https://cws.journals.yorku.ca/index.php/cws/article/download/10282/9371

Randall, W. L. (1995). *The stories we are: An essay on self-creation*. Toronto, Canada: University of Toronto Press.

Richardson, L. (1994). Writing: A method of inquiry. In N. K. Denzin & Y. S. Lincoln (Eds.), *Handbook of qualitative research* (pp. 516–529). Thousand Oaks, CA: Sage.

Riessman, C. K. (2008). *Narrative methods for the human sciences*. London, UK: Sage.

Robinson, J. A. (1981). Personal narratives reconsidered. *The Journal of American Folklore*, *94*(371), 58–85.

Roest, G., & Braidotti, R. (2012). Nomadology and subjectivity: Deluze, Guattari and critical disability studies. In D. Goodley, B. Hughes, & L. Davis (Eds.), *Disability and social theory: New developments and directions* (pp. 161–178). London, UK: Palgrave Macmillan.

Rogers, C. (2016). Intellectual disability and sexuality: On the agenda? *Sexualities*, *19*(5–6), 617–622. https://doi.org/10.1177/1363460715620563

Ross, K. (1994). Theorizing corporality: Bodies, sexuality and the feminist academy: An interview with Elizabeth Grosz (with Dr. Kwok Wei Leng). *Melbourne Journal of Politics*, *22*(1), 3–29.

Ruiz, F. J. (2017). The Committee on the Rights of Persons with Disabilities and its take on sexuality. *Reproductive Health Matters*, *25*(50), 92–103. https://doi.org/10.1080/09688080.2017.1332449

Sabatier, P., & Weible, C. (2017). *Theories of policy process*. London, UK: Routledge.

Sahi, M. (2015a). *Atita ka Sushkeraharu* (*Whistles from the Past*). Kathmandu, Nepal: Shilpi Saahitya Prtishthaan.

Sahi, M. (2015b). *Pidha bhitra ka chhatpati* (*A stressful struggle in sorrow*). Kathmandu, Nepal: Vintage.

Said, E. W. (1979). *Orientalism*. New York, NY: Pantheon Books.

Samowitz, P. (2010). A sexuality policy that truly supports people with disabilities. *Impact: Feature Issue on Sexuality and People with Intellectual, Developmental and Other Disabilities*, *23*(2). Retrieved from https://ici.umn.edu/products/impact/232/15.html

Sandowski, C. (1993). Responding to the sexual concerns of people with disabilities. *Journal of Social Work and Human Sexuality*, *8*(2), 29–43. https://doi.org/10.1300/J291v08n02_02

Schaaf, M. (2011). Negotiating sexuality in the Convention on the Rights of Persons with Disabilities. *Sur International Journal on Human Rights*, *8*(14), 113–131.

Schmidt, M. (1993). Grout: Alternative forms of knowledge and why they are ignored. *Public Administration Review*, *53*(6), 525–530. Retrieved from www.jstor.org/stable/977362

Schriner, K. F., Barnartt, S. N., & Altman, B. M. (1997). Disabled women and public policy. *Journal of Disability Policy Studies*, *8*(1–2), 1–6. https://doi.org/10.1177/104420739700800201

Schutz, A. (1972). *The phenomenology of the social world*. London, UK: Heinemann.

Shakespeare, T. (2000). *Help*. London, UK: Venture Press.

Shakespeare, T., Gillespie-Sells, K., & Davies, D. (1996). *The sexual politics of disability: Untold desires*. New York, NY: Cassell.

Sharma, J. K. (2007). *A study on the social status of women with disabilities*. Kathmandu. Nepal: Social Science Research Fund Secretariat.

Sherry, M. (2007). Chapter 1: (Post)colonising disability. *Wagadu: A Journal of Transnational Women's and Gender Studies*, *4*, 10–22. Retrieved from http://sites.cortland.edu/wagadu/wp-content/uploads/sites/3/2014/02/sherry.pdf

Shuttleworth, R. (2007). Critical research and policy debates in disability and sexual studies. *Sexuality Research and Social Policy*, *4*(1), 1–14. http://dx.doi.org/10.1525/srsp.2007.4.1.01

Shuttleworth, R. (2012). Bridging theory and experience: A critical interpretive ethnography of sexuality and disability. In R. McRuer & A. Mollow (Eds.), *Sexuality and disability* (pp. 54–68). Durham, NC: Duke University Press.

Shuttleworth, R., Russel, C., & Weerakoon, P. (2010). Sexuality in residential aged care: A survey of perceptions and policies in Australian nursing homes. *Sex and Disability*, *28*(3), 187–194. https://doi.org/10.1007/s11195-010-9164-6

Siebers, T. (2010). *Disability theory*. Ann Arbor, MI: The University of Michigan.

Spivak, G. C. (1988). Can the subaltern speak? In C. Nelson & L. Grossberg (Eds.), *Marxism and the interpretation of culture* (pp. 271–315). London, UK: Palgrave Macmillan.

Spivak, G. C. (1992). New nation's writer's conference in South Africa. *Ariel: A Review of International English Literature*, *23*(3), 29–48.

Spivak, G. C. (2010). Can the subaltern speak? In C. Nelson & L. Grossberg (Eds.), *Marxism and the interpretation of culture* (2nd ed., pp. 271–315). London, UK: Palgrave Macmillan.

Stevens, B. (2008). Managing unruly bodies: Public policy and disability sexuality. *Review of Disability Studies*, *4*(4), 15–22.

Stivers, C. (1993). *Gender images in public administration*. Thousand Oaks, CA: Sage.

Stivers, C. (2002). *Gender images in public administration: Legitimacy and the administrative state*. Thousand Oaks, CA: Sage.

Stone, J. H. (2005). *Culture and disability: Providing culturally competent services.* Thousand Oaks, CA: Sage.

Subedi, P. (1997). *Nepali women rising.* Kathmandu, Nepal: Sahayogi Press.

Tamang, S. (2000). Legalizing state patriarchy in Nepal. *Studies in Nepali History and Society, 5*(1), 127–156.

Tamang, S. (2009). The politics of conflict and difference or the difference of conflict in politics: The women's movement in Nepal. *Feminist Review, 91*(1), 61–80. https://doi.org/10.1057/fr.2008.50

Tanabe, M., Nagujjah, Y., Rimal, N., Bukania, F., & Krause, S. (2015). Intersecting sexual and reproductive health and disability in humanitarian settings: Risks, needs, and capacities of refugees with disabilities in Kenya, Nepal, and Uganda. *Sex Disability, 33*(4), 11–427. doi:10.1007/s11195-015-9419-3

Thapa, R. (2009). A renegade child of the hills. *Nepali Times.* Retrieved from http://archive.nepalitimes.com/news.php?id=16307#.WwOG9kgvzIU

Thapaliya, M. P. (2016). *A report on disability in Nepal 2016.* Sydney, Australia: Australian Himalayan Foundation. Retrieved from www.australianhimalayanfoundation.org.au/wp-content/uploads/2017/08/2016_Nepal_Disability_Report.pdf

Thomas, C. (1999). *Female forms: Experiencing and understanding disability.* Philadelphia, PA: Open University Press.

Thomas, M., Prakash, S., Hema, N. S., & Raja, S. (2002). Women with disabilities in South Asia. *A Journal of Women in Action, 2*(3), 45–52.

Traustadottir, R., & Harris, P. (1997). *Women with disability: Issues, resources, and connections.* Syracuse, NY: Syracuse University Press.

United Nations. (2006). *Convention on the Rights of Persons with Disabilities.* Retrieved from www.un.org/development/desa/disabilities/convention-on-the-rights-of-persons-with-disabilities.html

Waldman, H. B., Perlman, S. P., & Chaudhari, R. A. (2010). Hindu perception of disability. *The Exceptional Parent, 40*(7). Retrieved from www.questia.com/read/1G1-242754750/hindu-perceptions-of-disability

Warren, K. (2000). *Ecofeminism philosophy: A Western perspective on what it is and why it matters.* Lanham, MD: Rowman & Littlefield.

Watkins, J. C. (1996). *Spirited women: Gender, religion, and cultural identity in the Nepal Himalaya.* New York, NY: Columbia University Press.

Wehbi, S., & Lakkis, S. (2010). Women with disabilities in Lebanon: From Marginalization to resistance. *Affilia, 25*(1), 56–67. https://doi.org/10.1177/0886109909354985

Weick, K. E. (1995). *Sensemaking in organizations.* Thousand Oaks, CA: Sage.

Wendell, S. (1996). *The rejected body: Feminist philosophical reflections on Disability.* New York, NY: Routledge.

Wettenhall, R. (2003). The rhetoric and reality of public-private partnerships. *Public Organization Review, 3*(1), 77–107. https://doi.org/10.1023/A:1023000128175

Wilkerson, A. (2002). Disability, sex radicalism, and political agency. *NAWSA Journal, 14*(3), 34–57. Retrieved from www.jstor.org/stable/4316923

Wilson, E. O. (2002). The power of story. *American Educator, 26*(1), 8–11. Retrieved from https://msu.edu/~getty/powerofstory.pdf

Wilson, W. (1887). The study of administration. *Political Science Quarterly, 2*(2), 197–222. Retrieved from www.jstor.org/stable/2139277

Yami, H. (2010a). *People's war and women's liberation in Nepal*. Raipur, Nepal: Purvaiya Prakashan.

Yami, H. (2010b, March 21). Women's role in the Nepalese movement: Making a people's constitution (Opinion). *Monthly Review*. Retrieved from http://month lyreview.org/commentary/womens-role-in-the-nepalese-movement

Yanow, D., & Schwartz-Shea, P. (2014). *Interpretation and method: Empirical research methods and the interpretive turn* (2nd ed.). Armonk, NY: M. E. Sharpe.

Index

132   *Index*

emancipation from 86; government addressing 108; limiting women's life choices 108, 109; marginalizing the disabled 26–27; myth of non-sexual feelings 63–64; rates of 2; women's access to resources and 110
structural analysis: of disability policies 90–92; of narratives 86–90; procedures for 54
subaltern, definition of 43–44
subaltern group 107
subalternity 9, 62, 67, 70
syllogism analysis 48–49
symbolic interactionism 53
symbolic nods 55–56
sympathy, viewing disabled people with 69–70, 107

textual analysis *see* narrative analysis/ method
thematic analysis 54
typology of narratives *see* narrative typologies

UN Convention on the Rights of Persons with Disabilities (CRPD) 2–3, **81**, 82–83, 92, 103–104
United States: ameliorative programs 13–14; corrective programs 14; disability policies 11–12; disability programs 2
unjust social institutions 15
unmarried daughters, as goddesses 22–23
"us and them" binary relations 43

vermillion 61, 88
visual analysis 54

Waiba, Bishnu Kumari 68–72, 89, 98
women: access to resources 110; lack of unity among 67; psychological dependence on men 22; purity of 21; symbolic models as empowering to 22–23
women's beauty 38, 66, 97–98, 102
women's bodies, as hysterical 36–37
women with disabilities: as asexual/ genderless humans 105; colonized bodies of 94–95; desire for love 67–68; dispelling myth of asexuality 102; education of 67; employment situation 20; environmental disadvantages of 16–17; erotic feelings and desires of 60–61; experiences with doctors 65, 68, 73; as guinea pigs 73, 89, 93–94; imagery of 93; low marriage rate of 19; as marginalized 18; marital sexual aspects of 34–35; men's perception of 60; political and social power of 2; private vs. public life of 64; in public administration 16; reproductive rights of 12; sexist attitudes toward 1, 109; sexual and reproductive rights of 104, 109; social barriers for 2; social disadvantages of 16–17; social status of 18; socioeconomic status of 20; viewed with sympathy 107; *see also* persons with disabilities
writing, as process of discovery 52

For Product Safety Concerns and Information please contact our EU
representative GPSR@taylorandfrancis.com
Taylor & Francis Verlag GmbH, Kaufingerstraße 24, 80331 München, Germany

www.ingramcontent.com/pod-product-compliance
Lightning Source LLC
Chambersburg PA
CBHW050531270326
41926CB00015B/3165